# Year 8 English

# SPELLING WORKBOOK

## Weekly Targeted Practice Worksheets & Spelling Tests

### KS3 English
### Ages 12-13

# About This Workbook

Designed to make spelling more engaging for Year 8 students, this targeted workbook uses a **fresh approach** to help students **improve their spelling skills** over the course of the year.

Combining areas of spelling that KS3 students need to master with a range of topics that they actually find interesting, this workbook contains **39 units — one for every week of term for the whole school year**, each consisting of a **worksheet** followed by a **20-sentence spelling test**.

All the worksheets provide students with

- **Targeted lists of 20 words** to be learnt
- **Brief descriptions** of the **words** & the **spelling patterns** covered (where appropriate)
- **Bite-size tasks** to encourage them to evaluate their familiarity with, and their usage of, the target words

Additionally, each worksheet contains a **mix of self-contained sections** including

- **Cheat Modes** that reveal tricks to make learning the target words easier
- **Power Speller's Tips** that focus on relevant spelling rules (plus alternative spellings)
- **Easily Confused Spellings** & **Use the Right Words!** that draw attention to possible areas of spelling confusion
- **Notable Mnemonics** & **Brilliant Breakdowns** that provide further spelling-learning strategies
- **Useful Usages** which highlight commonly used phrases involving selected target words
- **Vocabulary Builders, Synonym Spotters, & Antonym Alerts** which point out connections between the week's target words and their meanings
- **Word Nerd Facts** which identify word origins & interesting facts about selected target words

At the end of the workbook, parents and teachers will also find

- **Suggestions** on how to **administer the spelling tests**
- **Full transcripts** for all 39 spelling tests
- **Suggested Answers to all** the **student prompts** included in the sections like the Vocabulary Builders, Synonym Spotters, Antonym Alerts, and Can You Think Ofs...
- **Indexes** to the spelling patterns and themes covered in the workbook organized by (1) areas and (2) units

# How To Use It

As the units are **self-contained**, they can be worked through **in order or** used for **focused practice**. In either case, we recommend that students

- Read the **Tips for Students** included at the start of the workbook
- Focus on **one unit a week**
- Take sufficient time to **absorb the information in the worksheets** and **complete the activities** in stages **BEFORE** attempting to learn the target words and doing the spelling test
- Identify the **spelling-learning strategies** they are **most comfortable with** & use them
- Revisit the worksheets as often as they need to

**Kindly note:** while **this workbook is a stand-alone volume**, its worksheets and tests **reinforce many of the words included** in our *Spelling Words for Year 8: 2,000 Words Every Student Should Know*.

Published by STP Books
An imprint of Swot Tots Publishing Ltd
Kemp House
152-160 City Road
London EC1V 2NX

www.swottotspublishing.com

Text, design, and layout © Swot Tots Publishing Ltd. First published 2022.

Swot Tots Publishing Ltd have asserted their moral right under the Copyright, Designs and Patents Act, 1988, to be identified as the author of this work.

All rights reserved. Without limiting the rights under copyright reserved above, no part of this publication may be reproduced, stored in a retrieval system, or transmitted in any form or by any means electronic, mechanical, photocopying, printing, recording, or otherwise without either the prior permission of the publishers or a licence permitting restricted copying in the United Kingdom issued by the Copyright Licensing Agency Limited, 5th Floor, Shackleton House, Hay's Galleria, 4 Battle Bridge Lane, London SE1 2HX.

Typeset, cover design, and inside concept design by Swot Tots Publishing Ltd.

British Library Cataloguing-in-Publication Data. A catalogue record for this book is available from the British Library.

ISBN 978-1-912956-42-5

# CONTENTS

**TIPS FOR STUDENTS**    4

**TERM 1**

**#1** WWI    5

**#2** That Doesn't Look Right...    7

**#3** As Dull As Ditchwater    9

**#4** Breaking the Law    11

**#5** From Benediction to Malodorous    13

**#6** Total Bedlam    15

**#7** Eureka!    17

**#8** Double Trouble    19

**#9** James Bond & Co.    21

**#10** Rags to Riches    23

**#11** Happy Endings I    25

**#12** Make an Impact    27

**#13** That Said...    29

**TERM 2**

**#14** Newton's Cradle    31

**#15** Hypercritical or Hypocritical?    33

**#16** Luck of the Draw    35

**#17** Justice is Served    37

**#18** Head-Scratchers    39

**#19** Kaput!    41

**#20** Before... & After    43

**#21** Happy Endings II    45

**#22** Short & Sweet vs Long-Winded    47

**#23** Body Language    49

**#24** Figuratively Speaking...    51

**#25** Claim to Fame    53

**#26** BOGOF    55

**TERM 3**

**#27** A Rapid Rise...    57

**#28** Que-ing Up    59

**#29** S is for Surprised    61

**#30** ...Or A Slow Decline?    63

**#31** Silent, but Deadly    65

**#32** It's Gone Viral    67

**#33** Going Without    69

**#34** Happy Endings III    71

**#35** A Fly in the Ointment    73

**#36** Say Cheese!    75

**#37** Stop the Presses!    77

**#38** T is for Trickery    79

**#39** That's a Proper Word?!?!    81

**NOTES FOR PARENTS & TEACHERS**    83

**SPELLING TESTS TRANSCRIPTS**    84

**SUGGESTED ANSWERS**    104

**INDEXES**    107

# Tips For Students: Ways To Learn New Spellings

By now, you'll know there are lots of different ways to help you learn new spellings — some of which work better for you than others. But, just as a quick refresher, here are some of the most common ones that you might have already used:

## I. Look, Say, Cover, Write, & Check...

This is where you
- Look carefully at a word
- Say it aloud to yourself (including silent letters!)
- Cover the word
- Write it down somewhere, and then
- Check to see if you got it right!

## II. Mnemonics...

This is where you come up with a funny sentence based on the letters of the word you're trying to learn. For example, to help yourself remember how to spell the word **stodgy** (s-t-o-d-g-y), you could come up with a sentence like

**S**top **t**alking **o**ver **D**an's **g**ran, **Y**olanda!

## III. Write Your Own Sentences...

This is where you think of a sentence of your own that contains the word and write it down. (We find silly or imaginative sentences work best for us!)

## IV. Pattern Spotting...

This is where you look at a list of words and try to find patterns of letter strings that words have in common. (Basically, it's like playing 'Spot the Difference' with words!)

## V. Listen, Spell, & Write...

This is where you get someone (e.g. your parent, teacher, a sibling, or even a friend!) to read the words out to you for you to write down. (Alternatively, you could record yourself reading the words, and then play your recording back to yourself!)

\* \* \* \* \* \*

If some of these techniques are new to you, why don't you give them a go?
You might find that they make learning spellings a bit easier.
It's not a problem if they don't, but there's never any harm in trying.
Plus, if you discover that there are several different techniques that work for you,
it will make learning spellings more varied!

## GOOD LUCK!

# #1 WWI

## This Week's Target Words!

| | |
|---|---|
| allies | dreadnought |
| armistice | entente |
| artillery | infantry |
| assassination | land mine |
| conscription | machine guns |
| contraband | munitions |
| convoy | pacifist |
| counter-attack | propaganda |
| doughboy | treaty |
| draft | U-boat |

## CHEAT MODES!

(i) Only the **last word** in this week's list **always HAS to have a capital letter: U-boat**.

(ii) Apart from 'armistice', all the words containing **doubled consonants** in this list **begin with 'a'**:

allies
artillery
assassination
attack (*in counter-attack*)

To remember these words, why not think of a sentence that contains them all? Possibly something like:

*The king's **assassination** prompted his **allies** to dust off their **artillery** for a counter-**attack**.*

**Bonus:** This will also remind you that **none of the other words contain double letters**.

## POWER SPELLER'S TIPS

(i) **All four words beginning with 'c' start with prefixes**:

**con**scription
**contra**band
**con**voy
**counter**-attack

(ii) When 'allies' & 'entente' are used as **names/parts of names**, they **need capitals** (e.g. 'the **A**llies' & 'the **E**ntente Cordiale').

## A. About these words...

The words for this week are ones that you might encounter when reading **historical accounts of** or **literature written during** the **First World War (1914-1918)**.

## B. Headcount...

Read all of this week's words carefully, then decide how many of them

You *definitely know*: _____

You *sort of know*: _____

You *haven't seen before*: _____

## C. The Top 5...

Before you start learning these words, copy out the **five** that you think will be the **trickiest** to remember:

_____

_____

_____

_____

_____

Why do you think these will be the most challenging for you to learn?

## VOCABULARY BUILDER

This list includes sets of related words:

- **Peace-related words:** armistice | entente | pacifist | treaty
- **Weapons:** artillery | land mine | machine guns | munitions

Can you think of any more groups? (*Clues: ships — specific names for soldiers*)

## BRILLIANT BREAKDOWN

**propaganda:** pro•pa•gan•da

(*Smaller units make words easier to learn.*)

## CAN YOU THINK OF...

A homophone AND a homonym for **draft**?

## TEST #1: Feeling confident you've learnt this week's words? Then give this test a go!

1. Until 1916, certain items such as rubber, cotton, and soap were deemed _____.

2. Following the _____ of Archduke Franz Ferdinand, war was inevitable in 1914.

3. Various tactical challenges during WWI led to a revolution in _____ techniques.

4. Siegfried Sassoon's poem "_____" vividly depicts the experience of trench warfare.

5. In 1917, the US government began to _____ men into the armed forces.

6. Relentlessly, German _____ wolf packs stalked their prey off the Irish coast.

7. With the outbreak of war, Britain's _____ machine went into overdrive.

8. After Germany violated Belgian neutrality, the _____ quickly deployed their troops.

9. The philosopher Bertrand Russell was a _____ who refused to fight.

10. Although part of the Triple _____, Britain was reluctant to join the war.

11. Women working in the _____ factories played a crucial role in the war effort.

12. '_____' was a nickname for a particular type of American soldier during WWI.

13. In November 1918, an _____, rather than a surrender, finally ended the carnage.

14. The creation of a _____ system reduced German attacks on Allied shipping.

15. _____ battleships were among the many craft that fought in the Battle of Jutland.

16. Men going "over the top" stood little chance against the enemy's _____.

17. The 1916 imposition of _____ gave rise to demonstrations in Trafalgar Square.

18. As a result of a _____ explosion, several soldiers were killed.

19. Following intensive negotiations, a multilateral _____ was finally ratified in 1919.

20. Flying too low, the French reconnaissance aircraft were hit by _____ fire.

**How well did you do?    Total Score: _____ / 20**

# #2 That Doesn't Look Right...

## A. About these words...

This week's list consists of words that we all **commonly misspell**: the words that you look at and think, 'Is that *right*?' (even when you've spelt the word properly!).

## B. Headcount...

Read all of this week's words carefully, then decide how many of them

You **never use**: _____

You **often use**: _____

You **sometimes use**: _____

## C. The Top 5...

Before you start learning these words, copy out the **five** that you think will be the **easiest** to remember:

_____

_____

_____

_____

_____

Why do you think these will be the most straightforward for you to remember?

## VOCABULARY BUILDER

This list contains **three words** that can be used as **BOTH nouns & verbs**:

camouflage | gauge | quarantine

Can you group the rest of this week's words accordingly? *(Clues: nouns — verbs — adjectives)*

## CAN YOU THINK OF...

A homophone for each of **gauge** & **kernel**?

## This Week's Target Words!

| | |
|---|---|
| atheist | inoculate |
| camouflage | kernel |
| concede | millennium |
| dilemma | omission |
| exhilarate | outrageous |
| gauge | pavilion |
| harass | perseverance |
| humorous | personnel |
| idiosyncrasy | quarantine |
| indict | supersede |

## D. Notable Mnemonic...

**G-A-U-G-E**

**G**igi **a**lways **u**ses **g**reen **e**nvelopes.

*(As you work through this book, try to come up with your own mnemonics to help yourself remember spellings that you find tricky!)*

## CHEAT MODES!

(i) In this list, the **two words** ending with an *eed* sound both have **the same final letter string 'ede'**:

conc**ede** | supers**ede**

**Bonus**: Think of how the words start so you don't mix up the soft 'c' with an 's':

**c**on**c**ede (c & c)
**s**uper**s**ede (s & s)

(ii) **Four words** in this list each contain **one pair** of **doubled consonants**:

dile**mm**a | hara**ss**
omi**ss**ion | perso**nn**el

(iii) Only **one word** has **two pairs** of **doubled consonants**:

mi**ll**e**nn**ium

## EASILY CONFUSED SPELLINGS...

**gauge** (to estimate)
**gouge** (to force something out brutally)

**personnel** (people who are employed in an organisation)
**personal** (belonging to a specific person)

## TEST #2: Find out how well you remember this week's words!

1. Scholarly research has shown there is often a _____ of truth in many legends.

2. A near-fatal experience may prompt even an _____ to turn to some form of faith.

3. To escape the unexpected downpour, we sheltered in a covered _____.

4. "Guerrillas continue to _____ the army in the mountains," noted the commentator.

5. Realising he'd been outmanoeuvred, the general was forced to _____ defeat.

6. Liam's _____ suggestion shocked everyone at the meeting.

7. To prevent the contagious disease spreading, patients were placed in _____.

8. A team of vets has been assigned to _____ all the cattle in the herd.

9. "Sales of electric cars will _____ those of petrol models in five years," predicted Ian.

10. Faced with a serious _____, Ethan asked his father for advice.

11. Only authorised _____ are allowed access to the bank's vault.

12. "I guarantee that a ride on that roller coaster will _____ you!" enthused Selma.

13. Lacking sufficient proof, the police couldn't _____ the suspect.

14. The company has apologised for the _____ of key information on its website.

15. A boom in bridge-building all over the world marked the _____.

16. Mimicking its habitat, the Solomon Island frog's skin provides it with superb _____.

17. After months of _____, the journalist tracked down the missing whistle-blower.

18. Edward Lear's *Book of Nonsense* is full of _____ limericks and illustrations.

19. To better _____ public opinion, the government will hold a referendum.

20. The pianist was as famous for her _____ of performing barefoot as for her playing.

### How well did you do?   Total Score: _____ / 20

# #3 As Dull As Ditchwater

## A. About these words...

The words this week are all **adjectives** that are **synonyms for 'dull' in some sense**.

**TIP:** Why not try using them the next time you want to describe something as 'boring'?

## B. Headcount...

Read all of this week's words carefully, then decide how many of them

You *sort of know*: _____

You *haven't seen before*: _____

You *definitely know*: _____

## C. The Top 5...

Before you start learning these words, copy out the **five** that you find the **most boring**:

_____

_____

_____

_____

_____

Why do you find these five words the least interesting?

## VOCABULARY BUILDER

Some of the words here are related:

- **Adjectives used to describe food:**
  bland | insipid | stale | stodgy

Can you come up with any other groups? *(Clue: adjectives to describe writing)*

## BRILLIANT BREAKDOWNS

**monotonous:** mo•not•on•ous

**pedestrian:** pe•des•tri•an

## This Week's Target Words!

| | |
|---|---|
| banal | prosaic |
| bland | stale |
| boring | stodgy |
| drab | tedious |
| dreary | undramatic |
| humdrum | uneventful |
| insipid | unimaginative |
| monotonous | unsensational |
| pedestrian | unspectacular |
| ponderous | vapid |

## D. Notable Mnemonic...

**S-T-O-D-G-Y**

**S**top **t**alking **o**ver **D**an's **g**ran, **Y**olanda!

## SYNONYM SPOTTING

**Be careful!** While all the words in this list mean 'boring' in some sense, they are **not all synonyms for each other** — nevertheless, there are some synonym pairs here:

- humdrum = prosaic *(i.e. everyday)*
- boring = humdrum *(i.e. repetitive)*

Can you see any other synonym pairs here? *(Clue: monotonous)*

## POWER SPELLER'S TIP

This list contains **five words** that all **begin with the same prefix 'un-'** but which **end in five different suffixes:**

undramat**ic**
unevent**ful**
unimaginat**ive**
unsensation**al**
unspectacul**ar**

## WORD NERD FACTS

The word **dreary** comes from the Anglo-Saxon word *dreorig*, which means 'mournful, or bloody'.

Similarly, **dull** comes from *dol*, which means 'stupid'.

# TEST #3: Think you've mastered your words for the week? If so, carry on!

1. Finding the new play too _____, the audience quickly became restless.

2. Thankfully, apart from hitting a bit of turbulence, our flight was _____.

3. "Don't be put off by the book's _____ cover — it's fascinating!" enthused Archie.

4. Without plenty of seasoning, you'll find that potato and leek soup _____.

5. Although Gordon's administrative job is _____, the pay is good.

6. Except for the odd weekend away, the lawyer led a very _____ life.

7. "Cole's suggestions are always _____; they're never exciting," she warned.

8. The architect's designs were rejected by the client as being too _____.

9. We were disappointed to discover that the new sitcom was incredibly _____.

10. Though that song has a catchy rhythm, its _____ lyrics let it down.

11. Reorganising your schedule is one solution to a _____ routine.

12. As Uncle Tony is allergic to most spices, his food is unavoidably _____.

13. Despite all the hype, the latest superhero movie couldn't be more _____.

14. The match was decidedly _____: neither side scored a single goal.

15. "A solid, but _____ performance," read a two-star review of the concert.

16. I'm not fond of landscape paintings; I often find them _____ and uninvolving.

17. For years, Professor Green's students have dreaded his _____ philosophy lectures.

18. To escape his _____ existence, Lorenzo decided to travel the world.

19. The characterizations in this new novel are quite _____; they all feel overfamiliar.

20. With its flat fields and marshes, the surrounding countryside was quite _____.

### How well did you do?    Total Score: _____ / 20

# #4 Breaking the Law

## This Week's Target Words!

abductor

abettor

arsonist

assassin

confidence trickster

cybercriminal

embezzler

fraudster

gangster

hijacker

kidnapper

murderer

phone hacker

pickpocket

poacher

smuggler

terrorist

trafficker

trespasser

vandal

## CHEAT MODE!

In this week's list, fourteen words end with the *er* sound, but **only two** of them end with **the final letter string 'or'**:

abduct**or** | abett**or**

**Bonus:** Helpfully, both these words **begin with 'ab'** <u>AND</u> they are the **first two words on the list** (which should make them super easy to remember)!

## POWER SPELLER'S TIP

**Three nouns** in this list end with the **suffix '-ster'**:

confidence trick**ster**
fraud**ster** | gang**ster**

The suffix **'-ster' forms nouns** that indicate a person is made distinctive by **a certain characteristic**.

## SYNONYM SPOTTING

As you might have suspected, this list contains several synonym pairs:

- abductor = kidnapper
- assassin = murderer
- smuggler = trafficker

Can you think of any synonyms of your own for words in your list?

## A. About these words...

All the words in this list are **specific nouns** that we use to refer to **particular types of criminals**.

## B. Headcount...

Read all of this week's words carefully, then decide how many of them

You *often use*: _____

You *sometimes use*: _____

You *never use*: _____

## C. The Top 5...

Before you start learning these words, copy out the **five** that you **most expected** to be included here:

_____

_____

_____

_____

_____

Why have you chosen these five words?

## D. Notable Mnemonic...

**V-A-N-D-A-L**

**V**era **a**lmost **n**ever **d**oes **a**ny **l**ifting.

## WORD NERD FACT

The word **murderer** is another word of Anglo-Saxon origin.

This time, it comes from the word *morthor*, which itself comes from *morth*, meaning 'death'.

## ODD ONE OUT

While being an **abettor** is an offence, it is still the odd one out in this list because an abettor is **a person whose crime is to help another person commit a crime**.

# TEST #4: See how many words you've got the hang of this week!

1. The police are considering the possibility that a _____ caused the explosion.

2. Bugs Bunny is by far my favourite cartoon _____.

3. Evidence suggests an _____ was responsible for the forest blaze.

4. According to our family legends, one of our ancestors was a tea _____.

5. The _____ terrified the passengers by threatening to blow up their plane.

6. "The ghost of a hanged _____ haunts these woods," whispered the gamekeeper.

7. Monique loves watching old _____ movies on a rainy Sunday afternoon.

8. In Renaissance England, a _____ was sometimes referred to as a 'cutpurse'.

9. To release the politician's child, the _____ demanded five million pounds in ransom.

10. The _____ responsible for slashing the *Mona Lisa* remains unidentified.

11. The focus of a nationwide manhunt, the _____ decided to turn himself in.

12. Ned Kelly, the infamous Australian bushranger, was a convicted police _____.

13. After years of stealing funds from his employer, the _____ was finally caught.

14. Yesterday, the president was gunned down by a masked _____.

15. "Any _____ found on this property will be prosecuted," read the sign.

16. Interpol have finally arrested that notorious drug _____.

17. Using a stolen identity, the _____ avoided paying taxes for years.

18. The rise of the mobile phone has created a new type of criminal: the _____.

19. Deploying viruses or phishing are two offences a _____ might commit.

20. Jo was charged with being an _____ for helping Mike with his scamming operation.

**How well did you do?    Total Score: _____ / 20**

# #5 From Benediction to Malodorous

## A. About these words...

This week, the words in the list are divided into two clusters:

**Cluster 1** (**benediction** ⇨ **benison**) are words beginning with **ben/e** which means **'well'** or **'good'**.

**Cluster 2** (**malady** ⇨ **malodorous**) are words beginning with **mal/e** which means **'badly'** or **'bad'**.

Ben/e & mal/e are used to form other words to add the meanings of well/good or badly/bad to them.

## B. Headcount...

Read all of this week's words carefully, then decide how many of them

You *definitely know*: _____

You *haven't seen before*: _____

You *sort of know*: _____

## C. The Top 5...

Before you start learning these words, copy out the **five** that are your **most favourite**:

_____

_____

_____

_____

_____

Why are these five words the ones that you like the most?

## POWER SPELLER'S TIPS

Both **ben/e & mal/e** are frequently identified as **root words**. However, **bene-** & **mal-** can be classed as **combining forms**, while **mal-** can also be classed as a **prefix**.

## This Week's Target Words!

| | |
|---|---|
| benediction | malady |
| benedictory | malaise |
| benefactor | malcontent |
| benefactress | malediction |
| beneficence | malefactor |
| beneficial | malfeasance |
| beneficiary | malice |
| benevolence | malignant |
| benign | malnutrition |
| benison | malodorous |

## CHEAT MODES!

(i) In Cluster 1, **only two words start with 'beni'**:

**beni**gn & **beni**son

(ii) Similarly, in Cluster 2, **only two words start with 'male'**:

**male**diction & **male**factor

(iii) **Two** of the three words ending with the *ents* sound are **'ence'** words:

benefic**ence** & benevol**ence**

while only **one** is an **'ance'** word:

malfeas**ance**

## SYNONYM & ANTONYM SOUP

Unsurprisingly, there are quite a few synonym and antonym pairs here including

- benediction = benison
- benefactor ≠ beneficiary

Can you see any other pairs here? *(Clues: illness — un/kind)*

## VOCABULARY BUILDER

Several sets of related words are in this list:

- **Health-related words:** benign | malady | malaise | malignant | malnutrition
- **Speech-related words**: benediction | benedictory | benison | malediction

Can you think of any more groups? *(Clue: types of people)*

## TEST #5: Feeling certain that you know your weekly words? If so, dive right in!

1. Mr Chan stood at the door beaming with _____ as his guests arrived.

2. The glorious spring sunshine was a _____ after endless winter skies.

3. In *Great Expectations*, Pip mistakenly believes Miss Havisham is his _____.

4. Judging from the _____ smell of the bins, food was rotting inside them.

5. As her father's only child, Chloe was the sole _____ of his billions.

6. With a look of unalloyed _____, the sorcerer disappeared in a puff of smoke.

7. A well-known literary critic's _____ can impact massively on a book's sales.

8. The donation of a generous _____ has saved our local museum from closure.

9. With the factory explosion came the release of _____ chemical fumes.

10. Paolo finds being bilingual _____ in all sorts of surprising ways.

11. It took the words of just one _____ to stir the crowd to rebellion.

12. Examining the company's records has revealed ample proof of _____.

13. Before the knights went off to war, Friar Francis said a short _____ prayer.

14. "Sadly, there's no quick fix to our economic _____," admitted the chancellor.

15. In revenge, the spiteful warlock invoked a _____ on the entire kingdom.

16. The remote village was struck down by an unknown _____; no one survived.

17. That the accused was a _____ of the highest order was borne out by the evidence.

18. Our previous mayor is fondly remembered for her numerous acts of _____.

19. Children are among those most likely to suffer from _____ in war-torn countries.

20. His _____ appearance completely belied the fact that he was a killer.

### How well did you do?    Total Score: _____ / 20

# #6 Total Bedlam

## This Week's Target Words!

| | |
|---|---|
| anarchy | mayhem |
| bedlam | misorder |
| chaos | misrule |
| commotion | pandemonium |
| disarray | rampage |
| disorder | riot |
| fiasco | tumult |
| furore | turmoil |
| havoc | unrest |
| maelstrom | uproar |

## CHEAT MODE!

This week, **only two words** (which also happen to appear consecutively) **each contain a pair of doubled consonants**:

co**mm**otion & disa**rr**ay

To remember these, why not come up with a funny/silly sentence that contains them? Possibly something like:

*The **disarray** caused by Derek's dynamic dancing resulted in a **commotion**.*

**Bonus:** This will also help you remember that **none of the other words** in your list have **doubled consonants**.

## POWER SPELLER'S TIP

**Two words** in this list contain the **tricky letter string 'ch'** which is **pronounced 'k'**:

anar**ch**y | **ch**aos

## EASILY CONFUSED SPELLINGS...

**bedlam** (a noisy, confused situation or place)
**beldam(e)** (an archaic word for an old woman)

## WORD NERD FACT

**Maelstrom** is a seventeenth-century Dutch word meaning 'whirlpool'.

## A. About these words...

This week's list is made up of **nouns** that are **synonyms for 'chaos' with slightly different shades of meaning**.

**TIP:** Why not try using them the next time you want to describe a situation as 'a mess'?

## B. Headcount...

Read all of this week's words carefully, then decide how many of them

You ***never use***:                    _____

You ***sometimes use***:              _____

You ***often use***:                    _____

## C. The Top 5...

Before you start learning these words, copy out the **five** that you think are the **most fun**:

_____

_____

_____

_____

_____

Why have you chosen these five words?

## BRILLIANT BREAKDOWNS

**anarchy:** an·arch·y
**furore:** fur·or·e
**maelstrom:** ma·el·st·rom
**pandemonium:** pan·de·mo·ni·um

## VOCABULARY BUILDER

This list includes sets of related words:

- **Chaos that is noisy:** bedlam | commotion | tumult | uproar
- **Chaos linked to citizens:** disorder | mayhem | pandemonium | riot | unrest

Can you think of any more groups? *(Clue: words of Greek/Latin origin)*

# TEST #6: Positive that you're now an expert on this week's words? Then wait no longer!

1. When the inmates' privileges were revoked, a _____ broke out in the prison.

2. The courtroom descended into _____ at the jury's verdict of not guilty.

3. Incensed protesters have gone on the _____ and are damaging property.

4. "This tropical storm is wreaking indescribable _____," said the reporter solemnly.

5. Last week, a heated debate in our history lesson ended in _____.

6. The _____ caused by a rat at Lady Delaware's luncheon is now legendary.

7. Disturbed by a _____ outside, Amit went to investigate.

8. Rosa's surprise party at the weekend was a complete _____.

9. The board has been in _____ since the company's disgraced director resigned.

10. Burglars ransacked our home, leaving it in complete _____.

11. "Widespread civil _____ will follow if this law is passed," predicted the analyst.

12. After twenty years of brutal _____, the dictator was eventually overthrown.

13. _____ reigned in France following the storming of the Bastille in 1789.

14. Anita stared helplessly at the _____ of her teenage daughter's room.

15. To prevent further _____ in the streets, the army has been called in.

16. A _____ has erupted owing to the proposed closure of our local primary school.

17. Famously, the premiere of Igor Stravinsky's ballet *The Rite of Spring* ended in _____.

18. The *Beagle*'s captain successfully steered her through the seething _____.

19. Britain witnessed great social _____ just after the end of the Napoleonic Wars.

20. Powerless to quell the _____, the emperor ordered the massacre of his citizens.

**How well did you do?    Total Score: _____ / 20**

# #7 Eureka!

## A. About these words...

This week's words are all **nouns linked to ideas, thoughts,** and **thought-processes,** each with a particular shade of meaning.

**TIP:** If you're unsure what a word means, look it up in your dictionary!

## B. Headcount...

Read all of this week's words carefully, then decide how many of them

You **haven't seen before**: _____

You **definitely know**: _____

You **sort of know**: _____

## C. The Top 5...

Before you start learning these words, copy out the **five** that you think will be the **least useful** to you when you are writing a piece of non-fiction:

_____

_____

_____

_____

_____

Why have you chosen these five?

## VOCABULARY BUILDER

More sets of related words!

- **Sciences-related words:** abstraction | concept | observation | conclusion | deduction | hypothesis | theory
- **Degrees of uncertainty:** conjecture | guess | hunch | hypothesis | speculation | supposition | theory

Can you think of any more groups? *(Clue: closed compound words)*

## This Week's Target Words!

| | |
|---|---|
| abstraction | guess |
| concept | hunch |
| conception | hypothesis |
| preconception | speculation |
| cognition | supposition |
| observation | theory |
| perception | brainchild |
| conclusion | brainstorm |
| conjecture | brainwave |
| deduction | inspiration |

## CHEAT MODES!

(i) **Three** of this week's words are **very close in spelling**. The slight **differences** between them are **highlighted in bold**:

concept
concept**ion**
**pre**conception

(ii) While ten words end with the letter string 'tion', **only one word finishes with the letter string 'sion'**:

conclu**sion**

## EASILY CONFUSED SPELLINGS...

**deduction** (reaching an answer or conclusion based on facts)
**induction** (a formal introduction)

## BRILLIANT BREAKDOWNS

**cognition:** cog•nit•ion

**supposition:** sup•po•sit•ion

## SYNONYM SPOTTING

Once again, you need to stay alert to **subtle differences in meanings** between these words — nevertheless, there are at least two synonym pairs here:

- conjecture = speculation
- brainwave = inspiration

Can you think of any synonyms of your own for words in your list?

# TEST #7: Feeling confident you've learnt this week's words? Then give this test a go!

1. "Now we've met, I realise my _____ of you was all wrong," admitted Freya.

2. "This groundbreaking project calls for a _____," the team leader declared.

3. To test her _____, the scientist performed a series of experiments.

4. The jury took very little time to arrive at the _____ that the witness was lying.

5. Children's experiences and social interactions help develop their _____.

6. The professor sheepishly confessed that his thesis was not actually his _____.

7. "No great discovery was ever made without a bold _____," he quipped.

8. About to give up in despair, Ned had a sudden _____.

9. Ezra's _____ that Sugarplum would win the steeplechase proved very lucrative.

10. "Talking about this problem in _____ won't solve it," grumbled Jorge.

11. Bert's _____ that I could help him could not have been more wrong.

12. "Without facts," retorted Mr Gradgrind, "you have nothing but _____."

13. Ivan spent hours trying to explain the _____ of quantum mechanics to me.

14. "Holmes, you truly are a master of _____," marvelled Dr Watson.

15. Your five senses help shape your _____ of the world around you.

16. _____ is often found in the most unlikely of places.

17. As a precaution, the doctor kept Maisie in hospital overnight under _____.

18. It only took Karl a matter of minutes to grasp Einstein's _____ of relativity.

19. The committee's report was useless as it was largely based on _____.

20. "You have absolutely no _____ of responsibility!" Ricky's mother scolded.

**How well did you do?   Total Score: _____ / 20**

# #8 Double Trouble

## This Week's Target Words!

| | |
|---|---|
| allocation | supplicant |
| embellishment | corrugated |
| hallucination | extracurricular |
| intelligentsia | surreptitiously |
| malleable | assassinate |
| asymmetric | connoisseur |
| commercialise | quintessential |
| consummate | attenuate |
| apportion | bloodletting |
| inopportune | intermittency |

## D. Notable Mnemonic...

**A-T-T-E-N-U-A-T-E**

**A t**iny **t**urtle **e**xplained **N**ewton's **u**npublished **a**rgument **t**o **E**ddy.

## CHEAT MODES!

(i) **Three** of this week's words contain not one, but **two pairs of doubled letters**:

> as**ss**inate
> con**ss**eur
> bl**oo**dle**tt**ing

(Note: assassinate, connoisseur, bloodletting)

(ii) **Four** out of the five words **beginning with 'a'** are immediately followed by **doubled consonants**:

> **all**ocation
> **app**ortion
> **ass**assinate
> **att**enuate

The one exception to this pattern is (ironically) the word **asymmetric**.

## EASILY CONFUSED SPELLINGS...

**attenuate** (to weaken or reduce something)
**extenuate** (to mitigate)

**allocation** (a particular amount of a thing for a particular purpose)
**collocation** (the way certain words are often used together)

## A. About these words...

**All** this week's words contain **at least one pair of doubled consonants: ll, mm, pp, rr, ss, or, tt**.

## B. Headcount...

Read all of this week's words carefully, then decide how many of them

You *sometimes use*: _____

You *never use*: _____

You *often use*: _____

## C. The Top 5...

Before you start learning these words, copy out the **five** that you think will be the **trickiest** to remember:

_____

_____

_____

_____

_____

_____

Why will these five be the most challenging?

## VOCABULARY BUILDER

There are several sets of related words here:

* **Adjectives used to describe objects/ materials:** malleable | asymmetric | corrugated

Can you think of any more groups? *(Clue: specific types of people)*

## POWER SPELLER'S TIPS

(i) **Both** the adjective forms **asymmetric** & **asymmetrical** are **correct**.

(ii) The adjective **extracurricular** can also be **correctly hyphenated** as **extra-curricular**.

## ODD ONE OUT

The **only adverb** here is **surreptitiously**.

## TEST #8: Find out how well you remember this week's words!

1. *The Merriam-Webster Dictionary* dates the first known use of '_____' to 1905.

2. Being _____ metals, lead and silver are easily hammered into shapes.

3. The _____ of wind and sunshine could adversely affect our electricity supply.

4. Scholars believe that the practice of _____ began with the ancient Egyptians.

5. During Queen Elizabeth I's long reign, numerous plots to _____ her were foiled.

6. _____, Fernando glanced about him before pocketing the gold necklace.

7. Plans are well underway to _____ this latest scientific discovery.

8. "Your _____ of the truth is not helping you," the headmistress warned sternly.

9. Much more must be done to _____ the devastating impact of extreme weather.

10. We encourage students to participate in _____ activities to broaden their horizons.

11. "I have no idea whether that figure was real or just a _____," he confessed.

12. In certain kinds of books, the _____ hero is tall, dark, and handsome.

13. Gigi learned that the _____ of tickets was on a first-come, first-served basis.

14. "She is a _____ liar. Never, ever trust her!" hissed Ahmed.

15. Falling on the shed's _____ roof, the hailstones beat out a thudding tattoo.

16. "To _____ blame at this stage is pointless," Titus advised.

17. Being a _____ of coffee, Uncle Jo can talk for hours on the subject.

18. Guaranteed to laugh at the most _____ moments, my cousin is a social liability.

19. Magnanimously, King Arthur granted the _____ sanctuary in Camelot.

20. It has been frequently observed that most people's faces are _____.

**How well did you do?   Total Score: _____ / 20**

# #9 James Bond & Co.

## A. About these words...

The words in this list are all related to the **super secretive world of spies** — whether they're real or imaginary.

## B. Headcount...

Read all of this week's words carefully, then decide how many of them

You **sort of know**: _____

You **definitely know**: _____

You **haven't seen before**: _____

## C. The Top 5...

Before you start learning these words, **imagine you are going to write a story about a spy**. Decide which **five** of this week's words that you would find the **most useful** and write them down here:

_____

_____

_____

_____

_____

Why have you chosen these five words?

## VOCABULARY BUILDER

Once more, there are sets of linked words here:

- **Code-related words:** cipher | cryptography| decoding | encryption

Can you think of any more groups? *(Clue: names of people engaged in espionage)*

## EASILY CONFUSED SPELLINGS...

**reconnaissance** (the obtaining of information — often military — about a place)
**renaissance** (rebirth or revival)

## This Week's Target Words!

| | |
|---|---|
| cipher | handler |
| counter-espionage | insider |
| counterfeiting | interception |
| counter-intelligence | interrogation |
| cryptography | mole |
| deceit | reconnaissance |
| decoding | recruitment |
| encryption | sabotage |
| espionage | safe house |
| forgery | secret service |

## CHEAT MODES!

(i) **Three** of this week's words **start** with the **prefix 'counter-'**:

**counter**-espionage
**counter**feiting
**counter**-intelligence

(ii) At the same time, **two** words are **identical apart from the prefix 'counter-'**:

**counter**-espionage
espionage

## POWER SPELLER'S TIPS

(i) **Two** words in this list are **'ei' words**:

counter**fei**ting | dec**ei**t

(ii) You can use the noun 'secret service' without capital letters in many cases.

If, however, you're referring to the division of the US Department of Homeland Security, **both words need capitals: Secret Service**.

## SYNONYM & ANTONYM SOUP

Unsurprisingly, there are a couple of synonym and antonym pairs here:

- counterfeiting = forgery
- decoding ≠ encryption

Can you think of any synonyms or antonyms of your own for other words in your list?

## BRILLIANT BREAKDOWN

**reconnaissance:** re•con•na•is•san•c•e

# TEST #9: Think you've mastered your words for the week? If so, carry on!

1. The young officer soon found that _____ intercepts was a painstaking job.

2. Having an _____ in the Persian camp ensured the Athenians' ultimate victory.

3. When his false identity was compromised, the agent fled to the nearest _____.

4. Julius Caesar used a form of _____ to convey secret messages to his generals.

5. The _____ of hostile aircraft was greatly facilitated by fitting radar sets into planes.

6. "_____ Officers Uncover London Spy Ring!" screamed the headlines.

7. The Enigma machine is among the most famous _____ devices in recent history.

8. A series of arrests convinced the group that they had been infiltrated by a _____.

9. In wartime, acts of _____ are most likely to be ascribed to enemy agents.

10. To this day, _____ is a priority for many countries.

11. The advent of drones has revolutionised how _____ is carried out.

12. _____ documents occurs in a shockingly large number of settings.

13. Some forms of _____ are no longer used, having been classified as torture.

14. For many people, leaking secret documents to the media is an act of _____.

15. "What do you know about the _____ of spies during the Cold War?" Vikram asked.

16. Slowly but surely, everyone was drawn into the spy's web of _____.

17. Close inspection proved the driver's passport to be a _____.

18. Another term that is used to refer to a _____ is 'case officer'.

19. A fascinating, new history of the _____ has just been published.

20. The possible evidence of _____ in an ancient Egyptian tomb remains disputed.

How well did you do?    Total Score: _____ / 20

# #10 Rags to Riches

## This Week's Target Words!

| | |
|---|---|
| bankrupt | poverty-stricken |
| beggared | straitened |
| cash-strapped | underprivileged |
| distressed | affluent |
| impecunious | flush |
| indigent | loaded |
| insolvent | moneyed |
| necessitous | privileged |
| pauperised | prospering |
| penniless | well-to-do |

## CHEAT MODES!

(i) **Two** words this week each **require a hyphen:**

cash-strapped | poverty-stricken

(ii) **One** word this week (which is also the last word on the list) **requires two hyphens:**

well-to-do

(iii) Plus, **apart from the prefix 'under-', two** other words are **identical**:

**under**privileged
privileged

## SYNONYM & ANTONYM SOUP

Once again, you have a list with quite a few synonym and antonym pairs!

- beggared = poverty-stricken
- affluent = moneyed
- pauperised ≠ prospering
- underprivileged ≠ privileged

There are other synonym & antonym pairs here. Can you spot them?

## BRILLIANT BREAKDOWN

**necessitous:** ne•ces•sit•ous

## CAN YOU THINK OF...

A homophone for **straitened**?

## A. About these words...

The words in this week's list are divided into two clusters:

**Cluster 1** (**bankrupt** ⇨ **underprivileged**) contains words to do with **people who do not have much/enough money.**

**Cluster 2** (**affluent** ⇨ **well-to-do**) contains words to do with **people who have an excess of/enough money.**

## B. Headcount...

Read all of this week's words carefully, then decide how many of them

You *often use*: _____

You *never use*: _____

You *sometimes use*: _____

## C. The Top 5...

Before you start learning these words, copy out the **five** that you **least expected** to find here:

_____

_____

_____

_____

_____

Why are you so surprised by these five words?

## D. Notable Mnemonic...

**A-F-F-L-U-E-N-T**

**A f**amished **f**rog **l**anguished **u**nhappily, **e**ating **n**utritious **t**ofu.

## EASILY CONFUSED SPELLINGS...

**indigent** (extremely poor)
**indigenous** (relating or referring to the people who originally inhabit a place)

**necessitous** (poverty-stricken)
**necessary** (essential)

# TEST #10: See how many words you've got the hang of this week!

1. With no money to pay her debts, the entrepreneur had to declare herself _____.

2. The hit TV series, *Downton Abbey*, follows the lives of a _____ English family.

3. Once they reach a certain threshold, _____ businesses often invest in expansion.

4. The firm has been declared _____ following its inability to repay its loans.

5. The Wall Street Crash of 1929 left innumerable families in _____ circumstances.

6. "Our _____ communities must be our top priority," declared the minister.

7. _____ or not, savvy shoppers are on the constant look-out for bargains.

8. If Pierre is feeling _____, he treats himself to an expensive dinner.

9. Upon her death, the film star was _____, despite earning a fortune in her heyday.

10. Karl Marx believed that the masses were exploited by the _____ few.

11. After decades of mismanagement, the country's _____ economy finally collapsed.

12. When they could not pay their rent, the _____ tenants were evicted.

13. Across the world, many _____ communities struggle to make ends meet.

14. Though sometimes _____, Ronaldo is happy in his chosen life as an artist.

15. Measures are being taken to stimulate business in economically _____ areas.

16. "I believe _____ citizens have an obligation to help others," she said stoutly.

17. Despite being a successful poet and playwright, Oscar Wilde died _____ in Paris.

18. Welfare systems are designed to help support _____ members of societies.

19. "She may not look like it," Jan whispered, "but, actually, that woman is _____."

20. The less _____ Romans, known as plebeians, struggled to gain political equality.

## How well did you do?    Total Score: _____ / 20

# #11 Happy Endings I

## A. About these words...

This week, all the words end with the **suffix '-ship'**.

When this suffix is added to a word, it **forms a noun**.

## B. Headcount...

Read all of this week's words carefully, then decide how many of them

You **definitely know**: _____

You **sort of know**: _____

You **haven't seen before**: _____

## C. The Top 5...

Before you start learning these words, copy out the **five** that you think will be the **easiest** for you to remember:

_____

_____

_____

_____

_____

Why do you think these five words will be the least challenging?

## VOCABULARY BUILDER

This list includes groups of related words:

- **Politics-related words:** bipartisanship | dictatorship | leadership | premiership | statesmanship

Can you think of any more? *(Clues: personal relationships — jobs)*

## EASILY CONFUSED SPELLINGS...

**kinship** (a relationship by blood)
**kingship** (the state of being a king)

## This Week's Target Words!

| | |
|---|---|
| apprenticeship | ownership |
| assistantship | partnership |
| bipartisanship | penmanship |
| censorship | premiership |
| courtship | professorship |
| dictatorship | readership |
| fellowship | scholarship |
| internship | showmanship |
| kinship | statesmanship |
| leadership | workmanship |

## CHEAT MODES!

(i) As **all** this week's words **end with 'ship'** (which is *really* easy to spell), even though some of the words *look* long, you only have to **concentrate on the first halves of the words**. For example

**censor**~~ship~~
**dictator**~~ship~~
**penman**~~ship~~
**scholar**~~ship~~

(ii) This week, **four** words contain **doubled consonants**:

a**pp**renticeship
a**ss**istantship
fe**ll**owship
profe**ss**orship

## POWER SPELLER'S TIPS

(i) By **removing the prefix 'bi-'** from the word 'bipartisanship', you can **add** yet another word to your spelling toolbox: **partisanship**.

(ii) You can use the noun 'premiership' without a capital letter in many cases.

If, however, you're referring to the former name of the Premier League (i.e. **the Premiership**), then it **needs a capital**.

## BRILLIANT BREAKDOWNS

**bipartisanship:** bi•part•is•an•ship

**premiership:** pre•mi•er•ship

## TEST #11: Feeling certain that you know your weekly words? If so, dive right in!

1. Luckily, the family possessed the documents proving their _____ of the property.

2. We all agree that Karim has the _____ skills necessary for this role.

3. More _____ laws to muzzle the press are being proposed.

4. After ten years of working together, the brothers dissolved their _____.

5. _____ programmes are often run by large companies and non-profit organisations.

6. The _____ of the Ring is the first volume of J. R. R. Tolkien's epic fantasy trilogy.

7. "Real political _____ entails both parties working together," observed Seth.

8. "Remember, the bonds of sibling _____ are sacred," the guru instructed.

9. My cousin Maria was overjoyed when she won a _____ to go to film school.

10. I stood in the ruins of the Roman villa, speechless at the _____ in the mosaics.

11. Anton's brother has been offered a research _____ at a famous laboratory.

12. Whether fairly or not, doctors have long been reputed to have poor _____ skills.

13. To boost its _____, that magazine is now offering reduced subscriptions.

14. "Do what you want!" Luc snapped. "This isn't a _____!"

15. Blake set up his own business having served his _____ as a plumber.

16. Although the group's act was undeniably polished, it needed more _____.

17. The president's _____ was tarnished by allegations of nepotism.

18. Famously, Hever Castle was the scene of Anne Boleyn and Henry VIII's _____.

19. Machiavelli's treatise for rulers on _____, The Prince, remains a controversial work.

20. Stephen Hawking's _____ at Cambridge was once held by Sir Isaac Newton.

**How well did you do?    Total Score: _____ / 20**

# #12 Make an Impact

## This Week's Target Words!

| | |
|---|---|
| alluring | effortlessly |
| Armageddon | enticingly |
| audacious | flawless |
| beauteous | hypnotic |
| beguiled | insidious |
| bloodbath | reckoning |
| charismatically | riveting |
| defiantly | tantalise |
| deliriously | thwarted |
| doom | vanquish |

## CHEAT MODE!

While several words here include the letter string 'ious', the **only word containing** the **letter string 'eous'** is **beauteous**.

## POWER SPELLER'S TIPS

(i) Only **one** word in this week's list **MUST always have a capital letter: Armageddon**.

(ii) Of the five **adverbs** in the list, **four** end with the **adverb-making '-ly' suffix**:

> defiant**ly** | effortless**ly**
> delirious**ly** | enticing**ly**

The **fifth adverb** needs the **'-ally' suffix**:

> charismatic**ally** ⇨ charismatic + ally

(**Note**: 'charismatical' is not a word.)

## WORD NERD FACT

The verb **tantalise** dates to the 16th century and is derived from *Tantalus*: a king in Greek mythology who was punished for his crimes by having water and food eternally move out of his grasp whenever he tried to have any.

## BRILLIANT BREAKDOWNS

**Armageddon:** Arm•aged•don

**charismatically:** char•is•ma•tic•ally

## A. About these words...

The words this week are a list of mixed **powerful words** (including **nouns**, **verbs**, **adjectives**, & **adverbs**) that are useful for writing about all sorts of things from battles to bewitchment!

**TIP:** If you want even more words like these, look this week's ones up in your thesaurus!

## B. Headcount...

Read all of this week's words carefully, then decide how many of them

You *sometimes use*: _____

You *often use*: _____

You *never use*: _____

## C. The Top 5...

Before you start learning these words, copy out the **five** that you think will be the **least useful** to you in your writing:

_____

_____

_____

_____

_____

Why do you think you won't find these five words handy?

## D. Notable Mnemonic...

**T-H-W-A-R-T-E-D**

**T**he **h**elpful **w**arlock **a**rrived, **r**eady **t**o **e**mancipate **D**emetrius.

## VOCABULARY BUILDER

There are several sets of related words here:

- **Attractiveness:** beauteous | flawless | alluring | hypnotic | riveting
- **Conflict-related:** Armageddon | bloodbath | reckoning | vanquish

Can you think of any more groups? (*Clue: captivation-related words*)

## TEST #12: Positive that you're now an expert on this week's words? Then wait no longer!

1. The smell of sausages sizzling _____ in the kitchen greeted a ravenous Ben.

2. The prisoner's attempted escape was _____ by an enterprising guard.

3. Smiling _____ at the cameras, the celebrity waved once and was gone.

4. With Ariadne's assistance, Theseus' _____ plan to kill the Minotaur succeeded.

5. _____ happy with her results, Mona called her parents immediately.

6. Acting under orders, the knights turned the peasants' protest into a _____.

7. The slow-swinging pendulum had a seemingly _____ effect on Ricardo.

8. Tempting the children with her gingerbread house, the _____ witch beckoned.

9. At the end of a _____ performance of *War Horse*, the audience cheered wildly.

10. For years, people believed that a nuclear _____ was an inevitability.

11. Tourists are always _____ by the history-laden atmosphere of our ancient city.

12. On such a hot summer's day, the ice-cold mountain lake was an _____ prospect.

13. We gazed on in awe as the figure skaters glided _____ across the ice.

14. Amidst the clouds of tear gas, the protesters _____ refused to move.

15. Try as she might, Miranda couldn't _____ her overwhelming fear of spiders.

16. "To free the _____ maiden, the warlock must be slain," the fairy told Sir Balin.

17. "Our enemy's day of _____ will come!" the defeated chieftain vowed to his men.

18. Jason's _____ dives earned him a gold medal at the Olympics.

19. "If you *will* _____ the cat, expect it to scratch you," Rahim told his sister.

20. As night set in, a sense of impending _____ descended over the besieged city.

How well did you do?   Total Score: ____ / 20

# #13 That Said...

## A. About these words...

This week's list is made up of a mixture of **phrases**, **adverbs**, and a **conjunction** that are used to **introduce**, **link**, **compare**, **contrast**, or **emphasise** ideas.

They are all extremely useful when it comes to **making your writing more formal**.

## B. Headcount...

Read all of this week's words carefully, then decide how many of them

You *haven't seen before*: _____

You *sort of know*: _____

You *definitely know*: _____

## C. The Top 5...

Before you start learning these words & phrases, copy out the **five** that you think you will use the **most often** in your writing:

_____

_____

_____

_____

_____

Why have you chosen these five?

## EASILY CONFUSED SPELLINGS...

**lest** (to avoid the risk of something bad happening)
**least** (the smallest quantity, extent, etc.)

**regardless** (in spite of; nevertheless)
**irregardless** (*NOT a proper word*)

**wholly** (entirely)
**holly** (an evergreen shrub or tree)

## BRILLIANT BREAKDOWNS

**admittedly:** ad•mit•ted•ly

**undoubtedly:** un•do•ub•ted•ly

## This Week's Target Words!

| | |
|---|---|
| above all | in theory |
| admittedly | inasmuch as |
| all told | insofar as |
| by the same token | lest |
| comparatively | likewise |
| conversely | on balance |
| hence | on the whole |
| in practice | regardless |
| in short | undoubtedly |
| in sum | wholly |

## D. Notable Mnemonics...

**C-O-N-V-E-R-S-E-L-Y**

**C**ora **o**bserved **N**ina's **v**icious **e**agle **r**ip **S**tuart's **e**iderdown **l**ast **y**ear.

**W-H-O-L-L-Y**

**W**ho **h**ad **O**mar's **l**iquorice **l**olly **y**esterday?

## POWER SPELLER'S TIP

Of all the adverbs in this list ending in 'ly', its addition to only **one** word has resulted in the **removal of the final 'e'**:

wholly ⇨ whol**e** + ly

## VOCABULARY BUILDER

Of all the words and phrases included here, **only one** is a **conjunction: lest**.

This conjunction is regarded as quite **formal or literary** and comes from the Anglo-Saxon *thy laes the*, meaning 'the less that'.

## SYNONYM & ANTONYM SOUP

Another list with several synonym and antonym pairs!

- in short = in sum
- by the same token = likewise
- conversely ≠ likewise
- in practice ≠ in theory

Can you think of any synonyms or antonyms of your own for other entries in your list?

## TEST #13: Feeling confident you've learnt this week's words? Then give this test a go!

1. "Today's meeting was, _____, an unmitigated disaster," grumbled Gerald.

2. "_____, I believe this project should go ahead," the mayor declared.

3. Our lawyer admitted to being _____ unprepared for the judge's ruling.

4. Her early poems deal with death; _____, her later works focus on love.

5. "Unfortunately, _____, this approach will be too time-consuming," noted Varsha.

6. The Romantic poets Byron, Keats, and Shelley valued feelings _____ else.

7. Serious repercussions will _____ follow the prime minister's latest announcement.

8. The critics called the book a triumph and the public seemed to think _____.

9. "_____," said Ali's instructor bluntly, "you must work much harder."

10. The collector was determined to purchase the portrait _____ of cost.

11. Punctuality is a desirable trait; _____, meticulousness is sought after.

12. "There is a rehearsal tomorrow, _____ I am aware," stated Oliver.

13. "_____, I don't think anyone has benefited from this," said Marina wisely.

14. The cuckoo is unusual _____ the female lays her eggs in other birds' nests.

15. "I'm no expert, _____; but I do know that that *isn't* linguine," sniffed Sita.

16. The disgraced head of the committee resigned _____ he be fired.

17. Currently, we have a glut of strawberries; _____, raspberries are scarce.

18. Two candidates happened to have the same name; _____ the confusion.

19. "It's a good plan _____, but it needs to be costed," Ashish observed.

20. _____, the article fails to make a persuasive argument.

**How well did you do?    Total Score: _____ / 20**

# #14 Newton's Cradle

## A. About these words...

All this week's entries are **nouns** you're likely to encounter in the **phenomenal world of physics!**

## B. Headcount...

Read all of this week's words carefully, then decide how many of them

You **never use**: ⎯⎯⎯⎯⎯⎯

You **often use**: ⎯⎯⎯⎯⎯⎯

You **sometimes use**: ⎯⎯⎯⎯⎯⎯

## C. The Top 5...

Before you start learning these words, copy out the **five** that you think will be the **trickiest** to learn:

⎯⎯⎯⎯⎯⎯⎯⎯⎯⎯⎯⎯⎯⎯

⎯⎯⎯⎯⎯⎯⎯⎯⎯⎯⎯⎯⎯⎯

⎯⎯⎯⎯⎯⎯⎯⎯⎯⎯⎯⎯⎯⎯

⎯⎯⎯⎯⎯⎯⎯⎯⎯⎯⎯⎯⎯⎯

⎯⎯⎯⎯⎯⎯⎯⎯⎯⎯⎯⎯⎯⎯

Why do you think these five words will be the most challenging?

## VOCABULARY BUILDER

A considerable number of this week's target words possess **scientific abbreviations**:

alternating current ⇨ **AC**
ampere ⇨ **A** | decibel ⇨ **dB**
direct current ⇨ **DC** | frequency ⇨ **F**
joule ⇨ **J** | newton ⇨ **N** | resistance ⇨ **R**

## WORD NERD FACTS

Three units of measurement here derive from the names of physicists: André-Marie **Ampère** (1775-1836) | James Prescott **Joule** (1818-89) | Sir Isaac **Newton** (1643-1727).

## This Week's Target Words!

| | |
|---|---|
| alternating current | diffusion |
| ampere | diode |
| antimatter | direct current |
| cathode rays | frequency |
| centre of gravity | half-life |
| centrifugal force | joule |
| centripetal force | newton |
| convection | refraction |
| decibel | resistance |
| diffraction | spectrum |

## CHEAT MODES!

(i) Of all the entries in the list that are made up of two words or more, **only one needs a HYPHEN: half-life**.

(ii) There are **five** entries here that **contain doubled consonants**:

alternating cu**rr**ent | direct cu**rr**ent
antima**tt**er
di**ff**raction | di**ff**usion

## POWER SPELLER'S TIPS

(i) Make sure you don't confuse the **UK spelling** of '**centre**' with its **US spelling** '**center**'.

(ii) Many of the nouns in this week's list start with **familiar prefixes**:

anti- ⇨ **anti**matter
con- ⇨ **con**vection
di- ⇨ **di**ode
re- ⇨ **re**fraction

What you may not know is that '**dif-**' is a **prefix** and is a **variant form of 'dis-'**:

dif- ⇨ **dif**fraction
dif- ⇨ **dif**fusion

(iii) **Two** words in this week's list start with the **combining form 'centri-'**:

centri- ⇨ **centri**fugal & **centri**petal

## CAN YOU THINK OF...

A homophone AND a homonym for **current**?

## TEST #14: Find out how well you remember this week's words!

1. When you observe something rotating, you are witnessing the effect of _____.

2. A conductor's _____ is affected by the material from which it is made.

3. The term '_____' can be used in relation to both sound waves and light waves.

4. In nuclear physics, '_____' describes the speed of radioactive decay.

5. The first atoms of _____ were created in 1995 by physicists working at CERN.

6. Apparently, microwave ovens use the same _____ band as Wi-Fi networks!

7. Varying wavelengths each undergo a different _____ upon entering a glass prism.

8. A clear example of _____ is the spread of perfume in the still air of a room.

9. The early televisions developed by John Logie Baird depended on _____.

10. Simply put, a _____ is the unit used for measuring the loudness of sound.

11. The closer an object's _____ is to the ground, the more stable it is.

12. Like many measurements, the _____ is named after a famous physicist.

13. If your electronic device is powered by a battery, it will use _____.

14. "I've forgotten the difference between a volt and an _____!" groaned Silas.

15. Within the International System of Units, 'N' is the symbol for '_____'.

16. While first used in optics, the term '_____' is now widely used in other contexts.

17. Did you know that _____ is defined as an apparent, rather than an actual, force?

18. Generally speaking, a _____ conducts an electric current in one direction.

19. In the average household, appliances such as fridges run on an _____.

20. One way heat can be transferred is through _____.

**How well did you do?    Total Score: _____ / 20**

# #15 Hypercritical or Hypocritical?

## This Week's Target Words!

| | |
|---|---|
| hyperacidity | hypoallergenic |
| hyperactive | hypochondria |
| hyperbola | hypocrisy |
| hyperbolic | hypocritical |
| hypercritical | hypodermic |
| hyperlink | hypoglycaemic |
| hypersensitive | hyponym |
| hypertensive | hypotaxis |
| hypertext | hypotensive |
| hyperthermia | hypothermia |

## CHEAT MODES!

(i) Of all this week's words, **only one** contains a **doubled consonant: hypoallergenic.**

(ii) All the words in this list **begin** with either **'hyper'** or **'hypo'**, so, once you've mastered these, even though the words may *look* long & difficult to spell, all you have to do is **concentrate on the second halves:**

> hyper**bola**
> hyper**thermia**
> hypo**dermic**
> hypo**taxis**

**Bonus Tip**: Why not try dividing the words into two groups: tricky halves & easy halves?

## VOCABULARY BUILDER

This list includes quite a few groups of related words:

- **Language-related words:** hyperbolic | hyponym | hypotaxis
- **Health- & Medical-related words:** hyperacidity | hypertensive | hyperthermia | hypochondria | hypodermic | hypoglycaemic | hypotensive | hypothermia

Can you think of any more? *(Clue: adjectives used to describe people)*

## A. About these words…

The words in this week's list are divided into two clusters:

**Cluster 1 (hyperacidity ⇨ hyperthermia)** are all words beginning with **hyper-**, which means 'beyond', 'above', or 'over'.

**Cluster 2 (hypoallergenic ⇨ hypothermia)** are all words beginning with **hypo-**, which means 'below' or 'under'.

## B. Headcount…

Read all of this week's words carefully, then decide how many of them

You *sort of know*:  _____

You *definitely know*:  _____

You *haven't seen before*:  _____

## C. The Top 5…

Before you start learning these words, copy out the **five** that you think will be the **easiest** for you to remember:

_____

_____

_____

_____

_____

Why do you think these five words will be the least challenging for you?

## EASILY CONFUSED SPELLINGS…

**hyperbola** (*in mathematics,* a type of curve)
**hyperbole** (exaggerated statements)

## ANTONYM ALERT

Unsurprisingly, the list contains a couple of antonym pairs:

- hypertensive ≠ hypotensive
- hyperthermia ≠ hypothermia

Can you think of any antonyms of your own for words in your list?

## TEST #15: Think you've mastered your words for the week? If so, carry on!

1. The disclosure of the minister's _____ has made his position untenable.

2. "Briony is _____ to criticism," Barry warned. "She doesn't take it well."

3. "One possible _____ of 'vegetable' is 'turnip'," explained Miss Jasper.

4. If you are _____, you should monitor your salt intake.

5. As Angela is _____, she always carries something sugary with her.

6. "Clicking on that _____ will take you to the website you need," Mo told Ivy.

7. On the night the *Titanic* sank, many of its passengers tragically died of _____.

8. "I have no idea what a _____ is," admitted Jan.

9. Malcolm, who is _____, suffers from abnormally low blood pressure.

10. Being _____, Naomi often finds it difficult to concentrate.

11. To avoid triggering an adverse reaction, use detergents marked '_____'.

12. _____ can be caused by eating spicy food.

13. People with _____ are given to diagnosing themselves with imaginary ailments.

14. '_____' is a literary term that describes how clauses relate to their sentences.

15. Severe heatstroke can lead to _____ in some cases.

16. Rihanna cringed as the nurse picked up a large _____ needle.

17. Many ads use _____ language to exaggerate the benefits of products.

18. "You're so _____! You say one thing and then do the opposite," snapped Fred.

19. Not wanting to be _____, I only pointed out one problem with her plan.

20. _____ enables extensive cross-referencing both within and beyond a single text.

### How well did you do?    Total Score: _____ / 20

# #16 Luck of the Draw

## A. About these words...

Once again, this list is divided into two clusters:

**Cluster 1** (**coincidental** ⇨ **serendipitous**) are all **adjectives** that mean **'lucky'** in some sense.

**Cluster 2** (**accursed** ⇨ **star-crossed**) are all **adjectives** that mean **'unlucky'** in some sense.

**TIP:** If you want even more adjectives like these, look this week's ones up in your thesaurus!

## B. Headcount...

Read all of this week's words carefully, then decide how many of them

You **sometimes use**:  ＿＿＿＿＿

You **never use**:  ＿＿＿＿＿

You **often use**:  ＿＿＿＿＿

## C. The Top 5...

Before you start learning these words, **imagine you are going to write a fantasy story**. Decide which **five** of this week's words you would find the **most useful** and make a note of them here:

＿＿＿＿＿＿＿＿＿＿＿＿＿＿

＿＿＿＿＿＿＿＿＿＿＿＿＿＿

＿＿＿＿＿＿＿＿＿＿＿＿＿＿

＿＿＿＿＿＿＿＿＿＿＿＿＿＿

＿＿＿＿＿＿＿＿＿＿＿＿＿＿

Why have you chosen these five words?

## D. Notable Mnemonics...

**F-L-U-K-Y**

**F**iona **l**iquidised **u**ncooked **k**ale **y**esterday.

**O-M-I-N-O-U-S**

**O**nly **m**ice **i**n **n**ifty **o**utfits **u**se **s**unscreen.

## This Week's Target Words!

| | |
|---|---|
| coincidental | serendipitous |
| destined | accursed |
| felicitous | calamitous |
| fluky | hapless |
| fortuitous | ill-starred |
| heaven-sent | infelicitous |
| karmic | jinxed |
| opportune | luckless |
| propitious | ominous |
| providential | star-crossed |

## CHEAT MODE!

This week, there are **three** words that **need hyphenating**:

> heaven-sent
> ill-starred
> star-crossed

**Bonus Tip**: All three adjectives have a strong **astrological** flavour through their respective uses of '**heaven**' and '**star**'.

## POWER SPELLER'S TIPS

This week, there are **six** words that contain **doubled consonants**:

> o**pp**ortune
> a**cc**ursed
> haple**ss**
> i**ll**-sta**rr**ed
> luckle**ss**
> star-cro**ss**ed

Of these, 'opportune' and 'accursed' have doubled consonants because they **begin with prefixes**:

> <u>o**pp**</u>ortune | <u>a**cc**</u>ursed

'**Op-**' is a **variant form** of the prefix '**ob-**' while '**ac-**' is a **variant form** of the prefix '**ad-**'.

## WORD NERD FACT

The word **serendipitous** was coined by the writer Horace Walpole in 1754 and derives from the word **Serendip**, which is a former name for Sri Lanka.

# TEST #16: See how many words you've got the hang of this week!

1. Karl regarded being fired as a _____ opportunity to change his career.

2. The mage was tasked with identifying a _____ day for the king's coronation.

3. It was purely _____ that we met at the train station that morning.

4. Jacinda waited patiently for an _____ moment to raise the issue.

5. The _____ defeat of the duke's forces left the city undefended.

6. "It was just _____ that I won," Claudia insisted modestly.

7. The adjective '_____' is now inextricably linked to Romeo and Juliet.

8. Glancing at the _____ black clouds overhead, Delia picked up her pace.

9. Lured by the sirens' song, the _____ sailor leapt into the sea.

10. A combination of _____ circumstances led to Jake's promotion.

11. After he was robbed for a third time, Niko began to believe he was _____.

12. In 1616, Sir Walter Raleigh set off on his _____ venture to find El Dorado.

13. In hindsight, it seemed _____ that they had left the day before the snowstorm.

14. Owing to an _____ similarity of names, Pierre was mistakenly arrested.

15. Many _____ climbers have failed to conquer Mount Everest.

16. Subsequent events would prove Bernard's choice of business partner _____.

17. A _____ discovery is one that is made by happy coincidence.

18. "I believe in _____ justice; what goes around, comes around," declared Lola.

19. With such formidable talent, Marcus was clearly _____ to succeed.

20. "Leave this _____ town," the lad urged. "You will not survive the night."

**How well did you do?   Total Score: _____ / 20**

# #17 Justice is Served

## This Week's Target Words!

| | |
|---|---|
| accusation | incarceration |
| advocate | innocence |
| arbitrator | jury |
| bailiff | justice |
| conviction | litigator |
| defendant | magistrate |
| expert witness | plaintiff |
| guilt | prosecutor |
| hearsay | sentence |
| imprisonment | verdict |

## CHEAT MODES!

(i) All **three nouns** in the list that end with an *er* sound conclude with the **letter string 'or'**:

arbitrat**or** | litigat**or** | prosecut**or**

(ii) **Five words** in this week's list contain **doubled consonants**:

a**cc**usation
baili**ff**
expert witne**ss**
i**nn**ocence
plainti**ff**

**Bonus Tip**: Both words that end with an *f* sound ('bailiff' & 'plaintiff') are spelt with **'ff'**.

## VOCABULARY BUILDER

As you might expect, this week's list includes several sets of related words:

- **Alternative names for lawyers:** advocate | litigator | prosecutor
- **Specific terms for people in a courtroom:** defendant | expert witness | jury | plaintiff

Can you think of any more? *(Clue: people who pass judgement)*

## BRILLIANT BREAKDOWNS

**arbitrator:** ar•bit•rat•or

**imprisonment:** imp•ri•son•men•t

## A. About these words...

All the words in this week's list are **nouns** that are linked to the **litigious world of lawyers & the law courts**.

## B. Headcount...

Read all of this week's words carefully, then decide how many of them

You **definitely know**: _____

You **sort of know**: _____

You **haven't seen before**: _____

## C. The Top 5...

Before you start learning these words, copy out the **five** that are your **least favourite**:

_____

_____

_____

_____

_____

Why have you chosen these five words?

## USE THE RIGHT WORDS!

**accusation** (a claim that a person has done something illegal)
**conviction** (a formal statement by a court that a person is guilty of an offence)

**sentence** (the punishment given to a person by a court, or the law)
**verdict** (a decision arrived at by an inquest, or, in a civil or criminal case)

## SYNONYM & ANTONYM SOUP

Another list with a few synonym and antonym pairs!

- imprisonment = incarceration
- guilt ≠ innocence
- defendant ≠ plaintiff

Can you think of any synonyms or antonyms of your own for other words in your list?

# TEST #17: Feeling certain that you know your weekly words? If so, dive right in!

1. The defence team have summoned an _____ to testify tomorrow.

2. "The coroner is expected to record a _____ of death by misadventure," stated Elias.

3. Unsurprisingly, the leaders of the coup were given life _____.

4. In Britain, minor cases are presided over by a _____, not a judge.

5. An impartial _____ was called in to settle the companies' dispute.

6. Through lack of evidence, the _____ has had to drop all the charges.

7. The judge reminded the _____ not to discuss the case outside the court.

8. "Will we be able to secure a _____ with this?" queried the detective.

9. "I believe community service is preferable to _____," opined the judge.

10. The _____ should have been awarded significant damages, but she wasn't.

11. "The importance of the presumption of _____ cannot be overstated," he declared.

12. One of the duties of a _____ is to serve court documents.

13. Many of the accounts that were heard in court last week were _____.

14. Having been a _____ for thirty years, Amit decided it was time to retire.

15. Despite her refusal to admit her _____, the police have a strong case against her.

16. In some countries, a lawyer is more commonly called an _____.

17. Calls are growing for the country's _____ system to be overhauled.

18. We were all shocked by the severity of Dan's _____.

19. The hearing has been postponed as the _____ is too ill to attend.

20. "This _____ of embezzlement is utter nonsense!" fumed the manager.

How well did you do?   Total Score: _____ / 20

# #18 Head-Scratchers

## A. About these words...

This week, the list is made up of **pairs of homophones**.

**REMEMBER: homophones** are words that **sound the same**, but which have **different spellings** and/or **different meanings** to each other.

## B. Headcount...

Read all of this week's words carefully, then decide how many of them

You **often use**: _____

You **sometimes use**: _____

You **never use**: _____

## C. The Top 5...

Before you start learning these words, copy out the **five** that you find the **least interesting**:

_____

_____

_____

_____

_____

Why have you chosen these five words?

## VOCABULARY BUILDER

This week's list includes quite a high number of groups of related words:

- **Mythology-related words:** augur | faun | satyr
- **Adjectives:** discreet | discrete | mean
- **Words that can be used as EITHER nouns or verbs:** censor | fawn | hoard | mean

Can you think of any more? *(Clue: literature-related words)*

## This Week's Target Words!

| | |
|---|---|
| auger | gild |
| augur | guild |
| censer | hoard |
| censor | horde |
| cite | mean |
| site | mien |
| discreet | rota |
| discrete | rotor |
| faun | satire |
| fawn | satyr |

## CHEAT MODES!

(i) **Four pairs** of words in the list this week are identical apart from **a single letter's difference**, which are all **highlighted in bold**:

aug**e**r & aug**u**r

cens**e**r & cens**o**r

**c**ite & **s**ite

fa**u**n & fa**w**n

(ii) **One pair** of words is identical apart from **a single additional letter**, which is **highlighted in bold**:

gild & g**u**ild

## EASILY CONFUSED SPELLINGS...

**censor** (an official who decides if part of a book, film, programme, etc. should be removed before it is made publicly available)
**censure** (an expression of severe criticism or disapproval)

**mien** (a person's manner or appearance)
**mein** (*in 'chow mein'*, a Chinese-style dish)

## USEFUL USAGE...

The word **gild** is commonly used in the phrase **gild the lily**, meaning 'to try to improve something that does not need improving'.

## WORD NERD FACT

The word **horde** comes from the Turkish word **ordu**, meaning '(royal) camp'.

# TEST #18: Positive that you're now an expert on this week's words? Then wait no longer!

1. Having lost, the defending champion had a decidedly disgruntled _____.

2. While they look similar, tangerines and clementines are two _____ fruits.

3. Students are expected to _____ evidence from multiple sources in their essays.

4. The store's closing-down sale attracted a _____ of bargain hunters.

5. As the incense in the _____ began to burn, a gentle fragrance filled the air.

6. Using an _____, the carpenter bored two holes in the piece of wood.

7. The young _____ stayed close to its mother, eyeing the rabbit curiously.

8. In the Middle Ages, artisans of the same craft would often form a _____ together.

9. My Aunt Nini is an avid consumer of political _____.

10. The _____ of treasure found at Sutton Hoo was the discovery of a lifetime.

11. Prior to publication, the _____ removed certain paragraphs from the novel.

12. "Wendy's so _____! She won't return my scooter," wailed Tina.

13. The proposed _____ of a new nuclear power station is being hotly disputed.

14. Climbing ever higher, the sun's rays seemed to _____ the distant mountain tops.

15. "Mr Tumnus" is the name of the _____ in *The Lion, The Witch and The Wardrobe*.

16. Hovering above us, the whirring of the helicopter's _____ blades was deafening.

17. "Your cousin is incapable of being _____; he's an awful gossip," complained Eric.

18. "I fear these events do not _____ well," she noted darkly.

19. According to the new _____, Nurse Maggie is on night duty this week.

20. A _____ is a mythological being which is half-man and half-goat.

How well did you do?    Total Score: _____ / 20

# #19 Kaput!

## This Week's Target Words!

| | |
|---|---|
| abseil | muesli |
| angst | Neanderthal |
| Bauhaus | poltergeist |
| Bildungsroman | pretzel |
| blitzkrieg | putsch |
| delicatessen | schadenfreude |
| doppelgänger | spiel |
| eiderdown | wanderlust |
| gesundheit | wunderkind |
| leitmotif | zeitgeist |

## D. Notable Mnemonics...

**A-N-G-S-T**

**A**fter **N**ora **g**roaned, **s**he **t**utted.

**S-P-I-E-L**

**S**ally's **p**oodle **i**s **e**xtremely **l**azy.

## CHEAT MODES!

(i) **Six** words in the list this week contain the **letter string 'ei'**:

abs**ei**l
**ei**derdown
gesundh**ei**t
l**ei**tmotif
polterg**ei**st
z**ei**tgeist

(ii) Contrastingly, only **two** words contain the **letter string 'ie'**:

blitzkr**ie**g
sp**ie**l

(iii) Only **two** words (which also happen to be **both the 'd' words**) contain **doubled consonants**:

delicate**ss**en
do**pp**elgänger

(iv) **Two** words contain the **same combination of vowels twice** in the same word:

B**au**h**au**s
z**ei**tg**ei**st

## A. About these words...

This week's list is made up of a **mixture** of words that come from **German** — a language that has given us quite a few interesting words!

## B. Headcount...

Read all of this week's words carefully, then decide how many of them

You **sort of know**: _____

You **haven't seen before**: _____

You **definitely know**: _____

## C. The Top 5...

Before you start learning these words, copy out the **five** that you **most expected** to find in this list:

_____

_____

_____

_____

_____

Why do you think these words are among the most likely to be included here?

## VOCABULARY BUILDER

Once again, many of this week's words can be grouped together:

- **Humanities-related words:** Bauhaus | Bildungsroman | leitmotif
- **The Paranormal:** doppelgänger | poltergeist
- **Emotions:** angst | schadenfreude

Can you think of any more? *(Clue: food)*

## WORD NERD FACTS

Several of the German loanwords here have interesting literal meanings in English:

Bildungsroman ⇨ 'education novel'
blitzkrieg ⇨ 'lightning war'
doppelgänger ⇨ 'double goer'

# TEST #19: Feeling confident you've learnt this week's words? Then give this test a go!

1. Staring at his spitting image, Fabio realised he'd just met his _____.

2. Did you know that _____ man was actually very intelligent and accomplished?

3. Our local _____ always stocks a wide range of imported cheeses.

4. When the class bully was finally punished, several children felt a sense of _____.

5. "You shouldn't _____ so much; it isn't good for you," advised Lauren.

6. Poor Igor cracked a tooth while eating a bowl of _____ for breakfast.

7. Consumed by _____, the two friends spent a year travelling across Asia.

8. In a literary work, a _____ can sometimes be difficult to distinguish from a symbol.

9. In 1940, Germany launched a devastating _____ against the United Kingdom.

10. One of the _____ movement's aims was to combine aesthetics with functionality.

11. Draped over the princess's bed was a deep red, silk-covered _____.

12. "To escape, the prisoner had to _____ down that sheer cliff," the reporter noted.

13. Having once choked badly on a _____, Lucille never eats them now.

14. "This poster perfectly captures the _____ of 1960s Italy," stated the art historian.

15. In 1920, a _____ to oust the Weimar Republic was attempted by Wolfgang Kapp.

16. Despite the salesman's enthusiastic _____, the customer was unimpressed.

17. When the German tourist sneezed, I couldn't resist saying, "_____!"

18. Many Victorian novels were written in the hugely popular _____ genre.

19. "I *swear* that rattling isn't the pipes. It's a _____!" hissed Mervat.

20. Aged only eight, Tiger Woods established himself as a golf _____.

**How well did you do?    Total Score: _____ / 20**

# #20 Before... & After

## A. About these words...

This is another week where the list consists of a **mixture** of words that fall into two clusters:

**Cluster 1 (antecedent ⇨ prologue)** are all words that entail the sense of **'before'** in some way.

**Cluster 2 (deferment ⇨ successor)** are all words that entail the sense of **'after'** in some way.

## B. Headcount...

Read all of this week's words carefully, then decide how many of them

You *never use*: _____

You *often use*: _____

You *sometimes use*: _____

## C. The Top 5...

Before you start learning these words, copy out the **five** that you think will be the **least useful** to you in your writing:

_____

_____

_____

_____

_____

Why have you chosen these five words?

## EASILY CONFUSED SPELLINGS...

**foregoing** (just stated or mentioned)
**forgoing** (going without something)

**precede** (to come before)
**proceed** (to begin; to carry on)

**precedent** (an earlier event viewed as a guide or example)
**president** (an elected head of a republic)

## This Week's Target Words!

| | |
|---|---|
| antecedent | deferment |
| antedate | descendant |
| beforehand | epilogue |
| foregoing | hindmost |
| foreshadow | postdate |
| preamble | posthumous |
| precede | post-mortem |
| precedent | rearmost |
| predate | subsequent |
| prologue | successor |

## CHEAT MODES!

(i) Only **one** word in this week's list contains **doubled consonants**:

su**cc**e**ss**or

(ii) In a similar vein, only **one** word requires a **hyphen**:

post-mortem

(iii) Of the **five** words that end with an *nt* sound, only **one** ends with **'ant'**, while the other **four** end with **'ent'**:

descend**ant**

anteced**ent** | defer**ent**
preced**ent** | subsequ**ent**

## POWER SPELLER'S TIPS

(i) Many of the words in this week's list start with **familiar prefixes, including:**

**ante-** ⇨ **ante**cedent
**ante-** ⇨ **ante**date
**epi-** ⇨ **epi**logue
**pre-** ⇨ **pre**amble
**pre-** ⇨ **pre**cede
**pre-** ⇨ **pre**cedent
**pre-** ⇨ **pre**date
**post-** ⇨ **post**date
**pro-** ⇨ **pro**logue

(ii) **Two** words in this list begin with **'fore-'**:

**fore-** ⇨ **fore**going
**fore-** ⇨ **fore**shadow

Some dictionaries classify **'fore-'** as a **prefix**, while others classify it as a **combining form**.

# TEST #20: Find out how well you remember this week's words!

1. One function of a play's _____ is to capture the audience's initial interest.

2. Despite her advisors' anxieties, the childless queen refused to name her _____.

3. "Don't _____ those cheques; my workers need paying today," instructed the foreman.

4. In a _____ search of the suspect's house, the stolen goods were found.

5. Stonehenge is among the sites that _____ the Romans' arrival in ancient Britain.

6. "The convoy's _____ ship will be most vulnerable to attack," cautioned the admiral.

7. Depending on its outcome, the trial may make legal history by setting a _____.

8. The meeting's _____ gave Luis a chance to improve his presentation.

9. To _____ the heroine's later demise, the writer kills off her dog in Chapter 1.

10. In the book's _____, the novelist hints at a forthcoming sequel.

11. "If we'd made reservations _____, we wouldn't be in this queue," grumbled Sunil.

12. Before the funeral can be held, the coroner must perform a _____.

13. On Saturday, a protest march will _____ the rally in the town square.

14. The events that led to the Boer War are outlined in the _____ pages.

15. To honour the town's heroes, the mayor has organised a _____ award ceremony.

16. "Here, the boundaries appear to _____ Roman roads," the archaeologist noted.

17. "I've discovered the bass violin was the _____ of the modern cello," remarked Gina.

18. There was no _____ to Jo's rant; she just started yelling.

19. Sitting in the _____ row, Ollie was finding it hard to hear the actors.

20. Our Aunt Cecilia claims to be a direct _____ of Queen Victoria.

**How well did you do?   Total Score: _____ / 20**

# #21 Happy Endings II

## This Week's Target Words!

| | |
|---|---|
| adventuresome | loathsome |
| bothersome | meddlesome |
| cuddlesome | quarrelsome |
| cumbersome | tiresome |
| fearsome | unwholesome |
| frolicsome | venturesome |
| gamesome | wearisome |
| gruesome | wholesome |
| irksome | winsome |
| lithesome | worrisome |

## CHEAT MODES!

(i) As **all** this week's words **end with 'some'** (which is *really* easy to spell), even though some of the words *look* long, you only have to **concentrate on the first halves of the words**. For example

**cumber**~~some~~
**lithe**~~some~~

(ii) In addition, **four** words are extremely **close in spelling**. The **slight differences** are **highlighted below**:

**ad**venturesome | venturesome
**un**wholesome | wholesome

## POWER SPELLER'S TIP

Of all the words in this list, only **two** follow the **'change the y to i'** rule with the **addition** of a **suffix**:

wearisome ⇨ wear~~y~~ + i + some
worrisome ⇨ worr~~y~~ + i + some

## SYNONYM & ANTONYM SOUP

Another list with a couple of synonym and antonym pairs!

- frolicsome = gamesome
- unwholesome ≠ wholesome

Can you think of any synonyms or antonyms of your own for other words in your list?

## A. About these words...

This week's words are all **adjectives** that end with the **suffix '-some'**.

This suffix is used to **form adjectives** and adds the sense of **'characterised by'**, or **'producing'**, to the base word.

**TIP:** Don't forget that '-some' can also be used to form nouns (e.g. four + some = foursome).

## B. Headcount...

Read all of this week's words carefully, then decide how many of them

You *sort of know*: _____

You *definitely know*: _____

You *haven't seen before*: _____

## C. The Top 5...

Before you start learning these words, copy out the **five** that you find the **most interesting**:

_____

_____

_____

_____

_____

Why do you think these five words are the most engaging in your list?

## EASILY CONFUSED SPELLINGS...

**lithesome** (having a graceful, thin, supple body)
**loathsome** (causing repulsion, disgust, or hatred)

## VOCABULARY BUILDER

Several words here can be grouped together:

- **Negative adjectives for people:** meddlesome | quarrelsome

Can you think of any more? *(Clue: positive adjectives for people)*

## TEST #21: Think you've mastered your words for the week? If so, carry on!

1. _____ people are often attracted to extreme sports.

2. With its high levels of fat and sugar, fast food is deemed _____.

3. "Mr Stevens is so _____! He always sticks his nose in," complained Zadie.

4. The monster's _____ appearance struck terror into the heart of Beowulf.

5. "Look at this teddy bear!" enthused Zara. "It's sooo _____!"

6. The singer's _____ smile was just one of the things her fans adored.

7. A _____ back injury has plagued Jumana for several weeks now.

8. With their _____ movements, tigers are beautiful, if deadly, creatures.

9. Feeling _____, the yachtsman braved the Indian Ocean's turbulent waters.

10. Protected by _____ hazmat suits, the firemen approached the blazing laboratory.

11. "This is quite a _____ development," admitted Beatrice.

12. One of Hercules' labours was the _____ task of cleaning the Augean stables.

13. The children squealed with delight at the _____ dolphins' antics.

14. At the thought of the _____ trek ahead through the jungle, Brett groaned.

15. Dylan increasingly found dealing with customers' complaints every day _____.

16. "I can't watch gory zombie films; they're just too _____," Vicki confessed.

17. Unsurprisingly, the long flight had left the children irritable and _____.

18. The _____ fairies flitted hither and thither, singing as they went.

19. "That new vegan restaurant's food is both _____ *and* tasty," raved Jim.

20. Staring at the mess, Cindy sighed at the _____ task of clearing it up.

How well did you do?    Total Score: _____ / 20

# #22 Short & Sweet vs Long-Winded

## A. About these words...

Once again, this week's words are all **adjectives** which are divided into two clusters:

**Cluster 1 (abridged ⇨ telegraphic)** all entail the sense of **'short'** in some way.

**Cluster 2 (circuitous ⇨ voluble)** all entail the sense of **'long'** in some way.

## B. Headcount...

Read all of this week's words carefully, then decide how many of them

You *sometimes use*: _____

You *never use*: _____

You *often use*: _____

## C. The Top 5...

Before you start learning these words, copy out the **five** that you think will be the **easiest** to learn:

_____

_____

_____

_____

_____

Why have you chosen these five words?

## VOCABULARY BUILDER

This week's list includes a few words that can be grouped together:

• **Words describing short, witty sayings:** aphoristic | epigrammatic
• **Adjectives sometimes used in relation to books:** abridged | concise

Can you think of any more? *(Clue: adjectives for talkative people)*

## This Week's Target Words!

| | |
|---|---|
| abridged | circuitous |
| aphoristic | circumlocutory |
| compendious | discursive |
| concise | garrulous |
| economical | loquacious |
| epigrammatic | meandering |
| incisive | prolix |
| laconic | rambling |
| pithy | verbose |
| telegraphic | voluble |

## CHEAT MODE!

Only **two** words have **doubled consonants**:

epigra**mm**atic | ga**rr**ulous

## POWER SPELLER'S TIPS

(i) This is another week in which quite a few of the words start with **familiar prefixes**:

circum- ⇨ **circum**locutory
con- ⇨ **con**cise
epi- ⇨ **epi**grammatic
pro- ⇨ **pro**lix

**TIP:** 'con-' is a **variant form** of 'com-'.

(ii) **One** word in this list begins with the **combining form 'tele-'**:

tele- ⇨ **tele**graphic

## EASILY CONFUSED SPELLINGS...

**economic** (relating to the economy or economics)
**economical** (giving good value)

**incisive** (being accurate)
**insightful** (being perceptive)

**incisive** (being accurate)
**decisive** (making decisions quickly)

## USEFUL USAGE...

The word **economical** is commonly used in the phrase **be economical with the truth**, meaning 'to deliberately withhold information, or to lie'.

# TEST #22: See how many words you've got the hang of this week!

1. The bride's father delivered a _____, yet heartfelt, speech.

2. A _____ argument with no clear direction will not convince readers.

3. _____ versions of Charles Dickens's lengthy novels are often used in classrooms.

4. Nathan's _____, monosyllabic reply infuriated his sister.

5. When summarising, be as _____ with words as possible.

6. Frustratingly, the witness's _____ account led nowhere.

7. Sula's witty brother always has an _____ response for everything.

8. Angie, our lovely but _____ neighbour, always wants to gossip.

9. "Be _____ — I haven't got all day!" shouted the impatient bureaucrat.

10. Melanie is far more _____ than her older brother, Micah.

11. My previous manager tended to address her staff in _____ bursts of words.

12. Normally quite _____, Edie was strangely silent yesterday.

13. My mother regularly uses the _____ saying: "Everything comes in threes."

14. "_____, paragraph-long descriptions of nature are boring," yawned Steph.

15. Notwithstanding its _____ start, Stan's speech was ultimately quite punchy.

16. Much praise has been lavished on the film for its _____ dialogue.

17. The mayoral candidate's _____ answers have won her new supporters.

18. Students can find a _____ breakdown of the syllabus in the course booklet.

19. If you tend to be _____, Twitter might be the wrong platform for you.

20. Mr Gradgrind's lecture to the students was as _____ as it was pompous.

...................................................................................................................................

**How well did you do?   Total Score: _____ / 20**

# #23 Body Language

## This Week's Target Words!

| | |
|---|---|
| aorta | lymph nodes |
| appendix | oesophagus |
| bronchi | pancreas |
| capillaries | pharynx |
| cartilage | sinews |
| cerebrum | tendons |
| cranium | torso |
| diaphragm | trachea |
| larynx | ventricle |
| ligaments | vertebrae |

## POWER SPELLER'S TIPS

(i) **Two** words in the list are **plurals** that are **formed without an 's' or 'es'**:

bronchi (pl. of bronchus)
vertebrae (pl. of vertebra)

(ii) In contrast, **thirteen singular nouns** in this list *can* **take 's' or 'es'** to form their **plurals**:

aorta ⇨ aortas
appendix ⇨ appendixes*
cartilage ⇨ cartilages
cerebrum ⇨ cerebrums*
cranium ⇨ craniums*
diaphragm ⇨ diaphragms
larynx ⇨ larynxes*
oesophagus ⇨ oesophaguses*
pancreas ⇨ pancreases
pharynx ⇨ pharynxes*
torso ⇨ torsos*
trachea ⇨ tracheas*
ventricle ⇨ ventricles

**Bonus Tip**: The plurals marked with an * have more than one correct plural form.

## D. Notable Mnemonics...

**C-R-A-N-I-U-M**

**C**hris **r**arely **a**ccepts **n**ew **i**deas, **u**nlike **M**aria.

**T-R-A-C-H-E-A**

**T**he **r**eally **a**nnoying **C**arl **h**id **E**liza's **a**rmadillo.

## A. About these words...

This week's words are all **nouns** referring to **particular parts of the human body**.

## B. Headcount...

Read all of this week's words carefully, then decide how many of them

You *haven't seen before*: _____

You *sort of know*: _____

You *definitely know*: _____

## C. The Top 5...

Before you start learning these words, copy out the **five** that you think will be the **trickiest** to remember:

_____

_____

_____

_____

_____

What makes these five words so challenging to learn?

## CHEAT MODES!

(i) **Two** words in this list are very **similar**. The similarity is **highlighted in bold**:

l**arynx** | ph**arynx**

(ii) **Three** words contain a **'y' with a** *short i* **sound**:

lar**y**nx | l**y**mph nodes | phar**y**nx

## VOCABULARY BUILDER

This week's list includes quite a few words that can be grouped together:

- **Types of connective tissues:** cartilage | ligaments | sinews | tendons
- **Heart-related words:** aorta | ventricle

Can you think of any more? *(Clue: the respiratory system)*

# TEST #23: Feeling certain that you know your weekly words? If so, dive right in!

1.  The _____ are key to distributing nourishment to different parts of the body.

2.  While running, Adrian tripped, tearing the _____ in his left ankle.

3.  The autopsy revealed a large tumour occupying much of the left _____.

4.  Two of the bullets fired at the soldier were lodged in his _____.

5.  Crushing a person's _____ will prevent them from breathing, which could be fatal.

6.  Falling off the ladder, Heba damaged some _____ in her knee.

7.  Swallowed food is carried by the _____ from the throat to the stomach.

8.  Inside the lungs, the _____ divide into smaller and smaller airways.

9.  Sound waves are created in the _____, nose, and mouth.

10. Our _____ is responsible for our thoughts, decisions, emotions, and character.

11. Type 2 diabetes is caused by the _____ not producing sufficient insulin.

12. Amazingly, a sparrow has more _____ in its neck than a giraffe!

13. The angrier Jackson grew, the more prominent the _____ in his neck became.

14. When Ola's _____ burst, she had to be rushed to hospital immediately.

15. With an inflamed _____, the actor was unable to perform that night.

16. If gored by a bull, a matador may incur serious wounds to the _____.

17. Dr Sanjay referred to Aaron's swollen _____ as 'buboes'.

18. To produce loud sounds, a singer has to control their _____.

19. Leonardo da Vinci advised studying _____, bones, and muscles to better depict the body.

20. Damage to the _____, the body's main artery, can lead to serious complications.

How well did you do?    Total Score: _____ / 20

# #24 Figuratively Speaking...

## A. About these words...

This week, the words are **the names of figures of speech** that you are almost certain to meet when you are **studying novels, poems, & plays**.

**TIP:** They are all extremely useful when it comes to **writing essays!**

## B. Headcount...

Read all of this week's names carefully, then decide how many of them

You *often use*: _____

You *sometimes use*: _____

You *never use*: _____

## C. The Top 5...

Before you start learning these names, copy out the **five** that you **least expected** to find in this list:

_____

_____

_____

_____

_____

Why do you find these five names so surprising?

## EASILY CONFUSED SPELLINGS...

**allusion** (an indirect reference)
**illusion** (a false belief or idea)

**bathos** (an unintentional change in mood from the serious to the trivial)
**pathos** (a quality evoking sadness or pity)

## BRILLIANT BREAKDOWN

**onomatopoeia:** on•o•ma•to•po•e•i•a

## This Week's Target Words!

| | |
|---|---|
| allegory | metonymy |
| alliteration | onomatopoeia |
| allusion | oxymoron |
| apostrophe | pathetic fallacy |
| assonance | pathos |
| aural imagery | personification |
| bathos | sibilance |
| dramatic irony | simile |
| hyperbole | synecdoche |
| metaphor | visual imagery |

## CHEAT MODES!

(i) **Two** words in this list are very **similar**. The similarity is **highlighted in bold:**

b**athos**
p**athos**

(ii) **Four** words end in a single **'e' which sounds likes a final *ee*:**

apostroph**e** | hyperbol**e**
simil**e** | synecdoch**e**

(iii) **Six** entries end in a **'y' which sounds like a final *ee*:**

allegor**y** | aural imager**y**
dramatic iron**y**
metonym**y** | pathetic fallac**y**
visual imager**y**

## VOCABULARY BUILDER

Predictably, the words this week can form quite large groups:

- **Devices related to sound:** alliteration | assonance | onomatopoeia | sibilance
- **Devices involving comparisons:** allegory | metaphor | pathetic fallacy | personification | simile

Can you think of any more? *(Clue: broad classifications for poetic use of language)*

## CAN YOU THINK OF...

A homonym for **apostrophe** and a homophone for **aural**?

## TEST #24: Positive that you're now an expert on this week's words? Then wait no longer!

1. The high levels of hissing _____ rendered the old recording unusable.

2. Chan's casual _____ to lunch made me realise just how hungry I was.

3. _____ occurs when the audience knows something that the characters do not.

4. _____ is used to evoke vivid pictures in a reader's mind.

5. Used effectively, _____ can conjure the typical sounds of almost any environment.

6. A silly phrase like 'as snazzy as a snail' might help you remember what a _____ is.

7. One of the most commonly used examples of an _____ is 'bittersweet'.

8. Homer's epic, *The Odyssey*, begins with the _____: "Sing to me of the man, Muse".

9. In Renaissance woodcuts, a grinning skeleton wielding a scythe is often the _____ of death.

10. Famously, *Animal Farm* is an _____ of the Russian Revolution and its aftermath.

11. Maintaining the balance between _____ and comedy in a play takes much skill.

12. Shot through with _____, Pedro's exaggerated account was wholly suspect.

13. A key challenge posed by tongue twisters is their frequent use of _____.

14. Employing 'the crown' to refer to 'the queen' is an instance of _____.

15. That poem's _____ brings it to life, eliciting the sounds of the bustling city.

16. "_____ is a term I constantly have to look up," complained Ayah.

17. The film's sudden switch from tragedy to comedy superbly demonstrates _____.

18. A phrase that illustrates _____ is 'the sullen wind'.

19. Despite favouring _____ over rhyme, the poem remains rhythmic and musical.

20. The _____ 'time flies' has become a cliché through overuse.

**How well did you do?    Total Score: _____ / 20**

# #25 Claim to Fame

## This Week's Target Words!

| | |
|---|---|
| celebrated | delinquent |
| distinguished | deplorable |
| eminent | discreditable |
| exalted | dishonourable |
| illustrious | disreputable |
| leading | ignominious |
| legendary | louche |
| prominent | notorious |
| renowned | opprobrious |
| reputable | scandalous |

## CHEAT MODES!

(i) **Two** words in this list are very **similar**. The similarity is **highlighted in bold**:

e**minent** | pro**minent**

(ii) **Two** words contain **doubled consonants:**

i**ll**ustrious | o**pp**robrious

(iii) **All five** words that end with the *ble* sound **conclude** with the **suffix '-able':**

reput**able** | deplor**able**
discredit**able** | dishonour**able**
disreput**able**

## SYNONYM & ANTONYM SOUP

As you might have expected, this list contains several synonym and antonym pairs:

* eminent = prominent
* exalted = illustrious
* renowned ≠ notorious
* reputable ≠ disreputable

Can you see any more pairs of synonyms and antonyms in this week's list?

## EASILY CONFUSED SPELLINGS...

**eminent** (notable, famous, or respected)
**imminent** (about to take place, or happen)

## A. About these words...

The list this week consists of **adjectives** which are divided into two clusters:

**Cluster 1** (**celebrated** ⇨ **reputable**) all entail the idea of **'good reputation'** in some sense.

**Cluster 2** (**delinquent** ⇨ **scandalous**) all entail the idea of **'bad reputation'** in some sense.

## B. Headcount...

Read all of this week's words carefully, then decide how many of them

You **definitely know**: _____

You **sort of know**: _____

You **haven't seen before**: _____

## C. The Top 5...

Before you start learning these words, copy out the **five** you think you will find the **most useful** in your writing:

_____

_____

_____

_____

_____

Why have you chosen these five words?

## D. Notable Mnemonic...

**L-O-U-C-H-E**

**L**ook! **O**utrageously **u**ndisciplined **c**hildren **h**urtling **e**verywhere!

## POWER SPELLER'S TIP

While several words in this week's list start with prefixes, **one sneaky word *looks* like it begins with a prefix, but doesn't:**

illustrious

This is because it comes from the Latin word *illustris* (which has no prefix).

## TEST #25: Feeling confident you've learnt this week's words? Then give this test a go!

1. To commemorate their _____ statesmen, the Romans built countless monuments.

2. "You should never buy a car from a _____ dealer," advised Julianna.

3. An _____ composer in his own time, J. S. Bach remains a giant of classical music.

4. The mere mention of the _____ pirate's name reduced the sailors to jelly.

5. "Such _____ behaviour cannot go unpunished," uttered the magistrate.

6. The _____ exploits of Robin Hood fascinate people to this day.

7. Soon after being found guilty of _____ financial activities, the bank closed.

8. "Your sister's _____ remarks are the talk of the town," Aunt Mavis said waspishly.

9. Opinions vary widely regarding the causes of _____ behaviour.

10. At various points in history, the theatre has been regarded as a _____ environment.

11. Cheetahs are _____ for their remarkable speed over short distances.

12. In 1588, the Spanish Armada suffered an _____ defeat at the hands of the English.

13. "Finding a _____ plumber is hard, but I know just the man," said Greg.

14. If you were asked to name a _____ fashion designer, who would you choose?

15. "_____ Hollywood stars are out in force tonight," gushed the gossip columnist.

16. "Constructive criticism is fine, but your remarks were utterly _____," said the writer.

17. Moving in the most _____ social circles, Lord Montague's self-importance ballooned.

18. The colonel's insubordination resulted in his _____ discharge from the army.

19. _____ scientists across the world are collaborating to find a cure.

20. "It's a shame such a _____ career is ending in disgrace," observed the pundit.

**How well did you do?  Total Score: _____ / 20**

# #26 BOGOF

## A. About these words...

All the entries in this week's list come from the **all-pervasive (and sometimes annoying!) world of advertising**.

## B. Headcount...

Read all of this week's entries carefully, then decide how many of them

You *sometimes use*: _____

You *never use*: _____

You *often use*: _____

## C. The Top 5...

Before you start learning these entries, copy out the **five** that are your **most favourite**:

_____

_____

_____

_____

_____

Why do you like these five so much?

## VOCABULARY BUILDER

There are several sets of related words here:

- **Blended words:** advertorial (advertisement + editorial) | infomercial (information + commercial)
- **Adverts often distributed by hand:** brochure | circular | flyer | handout

Can you come up with any other groups? *(Clue: words related to TV, radio, or streaming advertising)*

## WORD NERD FACT

The word **slogan** comes from two Gaelic words: *sluagh*, which means 'army' and *gairm*, which means 'cry'.

## This Week's Target Words!

| | |
|---|---|
| advertorial | handout |
| billboard | infomercial |
| blurb | jingle |
| brochure | launch |
| campaign | logo |
| circular | placard |
| commercials | promotional |
| endorsement | publicity |
| flyer | sandwich board |
| FOMO | slogan |

## POWER SPELLER'S TIPS

**FOMO** is an **acronym** for the phrase: 'fear of missing out'.

**Bonus: BOGOF** is another **acronym** and comes from the phrase: 'buy one, get one free'.

## EASILY CONFUSED SPELLINGS...

**handout** (a free piece of printed information that can be used to advertise something)
**hand out** (to distribute something)

**logo** (a symbol or design used by a business to identify itself)
**logo-** (*a combining form* used to show something refers, or is related, to words or speech)

## USE THE RIGHT WORDS!

**blurb** (a short promotional description)
**blurt** (to say suddenly)
**blab** (to talk foolishly)
**burble** (to speak at length in a confused manner)

## DID YOU KNOW THAT...

A person who carries a placard is called a '**placard bearer**'?

## BRILLIANT BREAKDOWN

**endorsement:** end•or•se•men•t

## TEST #26: Find out how well you remember this week's words!

1. Unless aimed at the right audience, an _____ is completely useless.

2. The team jogged onto the pitch, their t-shirts all bearing their sponsor's _____.

3. Marcus has designed an eye-catching _____ promoting his band's next gig.

4. At the train station, a huge digital _____ bombarded travellers with fast food ads.

5. The company is banking on their new advertising _____ increasing sales.

6. "If you're to succeed, your firm needs to invest in _____," the strategist remarked.

7. Appealing to people's _____ is a tactic regularly employed by advertisers.

8. Tara offered to help me distribute copies of a _____ for the new crèche.

9. Marketing experts are often consulted before the _____ of a new product.

10. "Have you seen that glossy travel _____ I had?" Emilio asked.

11. Occasionally, an _____ from a celebrity can backfire in unexpected ways.

12. It is ironic that many TV viewers switch off the moment an _____ comes on.

13. Coming up with a distinctive _____ is a lot harder than you might think.

14. Outside the cinema, a man held a _____ touting discounted DVDs.

15. "Enthralling! ... Unputdownable! ... Dazzling!" trumpeted the book's _____.

16. "If I hear that _____ once more today, I'll scream," threatened Samy.

17. Over the last decade, the number of online _____ has gone through the roof.

18. Each conference member was given a _____ listing local hotels and restaurants.

19. Running a _____ giveaway is good for raising brand awareness.

20. At one time, it was common to see a person wearing a _____ in the street.

........................................................................................................................

### How well did you do?   Total Score: _____ / 20

# #27 A Rapid Rise...

## A. About these words...

This week, all the words in the list are **verbs** which are **synonyms for 'increase'**, **each with a slightly different shade of meaning**.

**TIP:** Try using one of them the next time you want to say 'to get bigger / faster / larger / greater etc.'

## B. Headcount...

Read all of this week's words carefully, then decide how many of them

You **sort of know**: _____

You **definitely know**: _____

You **haven't seen before**: _____

## C. The Top 5...

Before you start learning these words, copy out the **five** that you think will be the **trickiest** to learn:

_____

_____

_____

_____

_____

Why do you think these five words will be the most challenging to remember?

## VOCABULARY BUILDER

Several groups of words are related here:

- **Size-related words:** burgeon | enlarge | expand | extend
- **Words that can be used as nouns as well as verbs:** mount | mushroom | snowball | surge | wax

Can you think of any more groups? *(Clue: number-related words)*

## This Week's Target Words!

| | |
|---|---|
| accelerate | intensify |
| accumulate | mount |
| appreciate | multiply |
| ascend | mushroom |
| burgeon | proliferate |
| enlarge | propagate |
| escalate | redouble |
| exacerbate | snowball |
| expand | surge |
| extend | wax |

## CHEAT MODE!

**Three** of the words here **containing doubled letters** are **tricky**:

a**cc**elerate | a**cc**umulate | a**pp**reciate

**Bonus:** All three **begin with 'a' PLUS** they appear **consecutively** as the list's first three words.

## POWER SPELLER'S TIP

The **antonyms** of **four** words in this list can be formed by **using** the **prefix 'de-'**.

In the first **three**, the **initial prefix is changed to 'de-'**:

**ac**celerate ⇨ **de**celerate
**ap**preciate ⇨ **de**preciate
**a**scend ⇨ **de**scend

In the **fourth** case, the prefix **'de-' is added with a HYPHEN**:

escalate ⇨ **de-**escalate

## USEFUL USAGES...

The verb **wax** is commonly used in **two phrases:**

(i) **To wax and wane**, meaning 'to alternate between increasing and decreasing'.

(ii) **To wax lyrical**, meaning 'to talk about something in a highly enthusiastic way'.

## BRILLIANT BREAKDOWN

**exacerbate:** ex•ace•r•b•ate

# TEST #27: Think you've mastered your words for the week? If so, carry on!

1.  Recent investment has caused the city's suburbs to _____.

2.  "Don't yell," advised Chloe. "It will only _____ the situation."

3.  "If left unchallenged, these rumours will continue to _____," warned Jed.

4.  Tragically, with every passing day, the death toll continues to _____.

5.  If Archie is to be selected for the team, he must _____ his efforts.

6.  As soon as the doors opened, the fans began to _____ into the venue.

7.  To _____ my project's progress, I asked Gita for help.

8.  Rising sales encouraged the entrepreneur to _____ his business.

9.  Since the painting's value had begun to _____, the collector decided to insure it.

10. Overnight, the weeds in the garden seemed to _____ as if by magic.

11. Tia's criticism only served to _____ Ravi's stubbornness.

12. "I don't know how I've managed to _____ all these plastic bags," moaned Ted.

13. "There are signs this trend will _____," observed the analyst.

14. "To accommodate cruise ships, we'll have to _____ the port," the engineer noted.

15. We're delighted that new shops are starting to _____ in our city centre.

16. Fearing the peaceful protest would _____ into a riot, we decided to leave.

17. The moon is said to _____ as it transitions from a crescent to a disc.

18. Since Gavin was having such a great time, he decided to _____ his stay.

19. In record time, Sebastian managed to _____ to the rank of major.

20. "Speculations about what caused this continue to _____," announced the reporter.

How well did you do?    Total Score: _____ / 20

# #28 Que-ing Up

## This Week's Target Words!

| | |
|---|---|
| appliqué | masque |
| arabesque | mystique |
| baroque | oblique |
| barque | picaresque |
| burlesque | picturesque |
| communiqué | pique |
| critique | plaque |
| goblinesque | risqué |
| grotesque | statuesque |
| marque | torque |

## D. Notable Mnemonic...

**B-A-R-Q-U-E**

**B**ob **a**te **r**aw **q**uinoa **u**ntil **E**aster.

## CHEAT MODES!

(i) **Only one** word that contains an 's' does **NOT end** with **'sque'**:

mystique

(ii) **Two pairs** of words are **almost identical**, each with only **one letter's difference**:

bar**o**que & bar**q**ue
mar**q**ue & ma**s**que

(iii) **Three** words here **end** with an **é**:

appliqu**é** | communiqu**é** | risqu**é**

## POWER SPELLER'S TIP

When used to refer to 'a neck ornament formed of a twisted metal band', the word **torque** can also be correctly spelt **torc**.

## EASILY CONFUSED SPELLINGS...

**marque** (*esp. in cars*, a make or brand)
**marquee** (a very large tent)

**mystique** (a mysterious quality)
**mystic** (*in religion*, a person who devotes their life to prayer or meditation)

## A. About these words...

This week's list is made up of a **mixture** of tricky **nouns, adjectives, & verbs** which all **end with the letter string 'que'**.

## B. Headcount...

Read all of this week's words carefully, then decide how many of them

You **sometimes use**: _____

You **often use**: _____

You **never use**: _____

## C. The Top 5...

Before you start learning these words, copy out the **five** that you think will be the **easiest** for you to remember:

_____

_____

_____

_____

_____

Why do you think these five words will be the least challenging to learn?

## VOCABULARY BUILDER

This list includes several sets of related words:

- **Dance:** arabesque | masque
- **Art & Architecture:** baroque | grotesque
- **Literature:** barque | burlesque | critique | masque | picaresque

Can you see any more sets here? (*Clue: nouns with multiple definitions*)

## CAN YOU THINK OF...

A homophone for each of **barque & pique**?

## WORD NERD FACT

**Goblinesque**, meaning 'like a goblin', was **coined in the late nineteenth century**.

# TEST #28: See how many words you've got the hang of this week!

1.  With a _____ grin, the warlock began to cast his malicious spell.

2.  The word '_____' can be used to refer to a specific kind of sailing ship.

3.  Yesterday's newspaper carried a scathing _____ of the government's new policy.

4.  Famously, Mercedes-Benz is a _____ associated with both luxury cars and F1 racing.

5.  Standing motionless in the shallow water, the heron cut a _____ figure.

6.  To '_____' something is to parody or comically imitate it.

7.  I far prefer direct disapproval to _____ criticism.

8.  Put simply, _____ involves sewing bits of fabric onto a larger piece of cloth.

9.  Last summer, we rented a _____ thatched cottage in Cornwall.

10. As the _____ creature began to emerge from the shadows, Petronella froze.

11. Owen's grandmother has never found his _____ anecdotes amusing.

12. Alicia's attempt at an _____ was short-lived; she tripped over almost immediately.

13. Renaissance rulers capitalised on the _____ surrounding the idea of monarchy.

14. Flossing regularly can help reduce the build-up of _____.

15. The heavier the vehicle, the greater its engine's _____ needs to be.

16. The _____ was a form of dramatic entertainment in sixteenth-century England.

17. Ornamentation and grandeur are two key characteristics of _____ architecture.

18. In a fit of _____, Stefan stormed out of the room.

19. We are expecting the War Office to issue a _____ in the next few hours.

20. A _____ novel is commonly formed of a series of entertaining episodes.

How well did you do?     Total Score: _____ / 20

# #29 S is for Surprised

## A. About these words...

This week, all the words in the list are a **mixture of adjectives** and **verbs** which are closely **linked to the feeling of surprise**.

## B. Headcount...

Read all of this week's words carefully, then decide how many of them

You **haven't seen before**: _____

You **sort of know**: _____

You **definitely know**: _____

## C. The Top 5...

Before you start learning these words, copy out the **five** that you find the **most surprising** to see here:

_____

_____

_____

_____

_____

Why have you chosen these five words?

## D. Notable Mnemonic...

**A-G-A-P-E**

**A**lice's **g**arrulous **a**unt **p**roved **e**ntertaining.

## VOCABULARY BUILDER

Predictably, several of this week's words form smaller groups:

- **Speech-related words:** dumbfounded | dumbstruck | speechless | stunned

Can you think of any more? *(Clue: face-related words)*

## This Week's Target Words!

| | |
|---|---|
| agape | goggle-eyed |
| astounded | nonplussed |
| benumbed | shell-shocked |
| confounded | speechless |
| dazed | staggered |
| dumbfounded | startled |
| dumbstruck | stunned |
| flabbergasted | stupefied |
| floored | thunderstruck |
| flummoxed | wide-eyed |

## CHEAT MODES!

(i) **Three** words here **need HYPHENS:**

goggle-eyed | shell-shocked | wide-eyed

(ii) **Two** words **begin in the same way:**

**dumb**founded | **dumb**struck

(iii) **Two pairs** of words each **end in the same way:**

dumb**struck** | thunder**struck**
goggle-**eyed** | wide-**eyed**

(iv) **Three** words **end** with the **letter string 'ounded':**

ast**ounded** | conf**ounded** | dumbf**ounded**

## POWER SPELLER'S TIPS

(i) **Five** words contain **doubled consonants** that are **NOT** the result of **adding a suffix:**

fla**bb**ergasted | flu**mm**oxed
go**gg**le-eyed | shell-shocked | sta**gg**ered

(ii) **Two** words contain **doubled consonants as a result of adding a suffix:**

nonplu**ss**ed (nonplus + ed)
stu**nn**ed (stun + ed)

(iii) **One** word has a **doubled consonant because of the suffix itself:**

speechle**ss** (speech + le**ss**)

## HOMOGRAPH HASSLE...

**agape** (*adj.* wide open)
**agape** (*in religion*, *n.* brotherly love)

## TEST #29: Feeling certain that you know your weekly words? If so, dive right in!

1. Discovering that she'd won, Betty was too _____ to speak.

2. With mouth _____, Callum stood stock-still, overcome with awe.

3. Camilla, who usually has an answer for everything, was _____ into silence.

4. Looking _____ and disappointed, the defeated boxer left the ring.

5. _____ by the actor's bizarre behaviour, the audience fell silent.

6. Astrophysicists have been _____ by the results of the experiment.

7. Melinda laughed at the _____ expressions on all our faces.

8. The news of the athlete's sudden retirement has left many pundits _____.

9. "You look utterly _____!" Trudi exclaimed. "What's happened?"

10. Krista sat motionless in her chair, completely _____ by her sister's tirade.

11. "'_____' doesn't begin to describe how I feel," Luke said mournfully.

12. When I received the bill, I was _____ by how much I'd been charged.

13. "Prepare to be _____!" promised the film's rave review.

14. "Don't just sit there _____!" yelled Zenobia. "Do something!"

15. "Residents remain _____ by the devastation here," the reporter stated.

16. The story follows the fortunes of a _____ soldier on his return from the trenches.

17. Several of us were _____ by the final question in the maths exam.

18. "I must admit to being _____ by Rick's apology," Vera acknowledged.

19. _____ by the sudden noise, the cows began stampeding in every direction.

20. Tristram didn't know what to say; the question had completely _____ him.

How well did you do?    Total Score: _____ / 20

# #30 ...Or A Slow Decline?

## This Week's Target Words!

| | |
|---|---|
| abate | downsize |
| collapse | dwindle |
| contract | ebb |
| debase | plummet |
| decimate | plunge |
| degenerate | recede |
| deplete | shrink |
| deteriorate | slump |
| devolve | tumble |
| downscale | wane |

## CHEAT MODE!

Of all the words containing more than one vowel, **two** words **each use** the **same vowel three times over:**

d**e**pl**e**t**e** | r**e**c**e**d**e**

## EASILY CONFUSED SPELLINGS...

**deplete** (to greatly reduce in number, quantity, etc.)
**delete** (to rub out or remove something)
**recede** (to move further away or to go back)
**re-cede** (to cede again)
**reseed** (to sow land again, especially with grass)

## USEFUL USAGE...

The way we use the verb **decimate** has changed. It was **originally** used to mean **'to remove or take one in every ten'**. It is **now** used to mean **'to destroy a large part of something'**.

## WORD NERD FACT

The verb **dwindle** comes from the Anglo-Saxon word *dwinan*, meaning 'to fade'.

## A. About these words...

The words in this week's list are **verbs** that are **synonyms for 'decrease', each with a slightly different shade of meaning**.

**TIP:** Why not compare these verbs to the ones in **#27: A Rapid Rise...** and see if you can make some **antonym pairs**?

## B. Headcount...

Read all of this week's words carefully, then decide how many of them

You *never use*: _____

You *sometimes use*: _____

You *often use*: _____

## C. The Top 5...

Before you start learning these words, copy out the **five** that you find the **most boring**:

_____

_____

_____

_____

_____

Why have you chosen these five words?

## VOCABULARY BUILDER

Several groups of words are related here:

- **Stock market-related words:** collapse | plummet | plunge | tumble
- **Economy-related words:** contract | shrink | slump

Can you think of any more? *(Clue: words related to businesses)*

## SYNONYM SPOTTING

Unsurprisingly, this list contains quite a few synonym pairs!

- contract = shrink
- degenerate = devolve

Can you see any other synonym pairs here?

## TEST #30: Positive that you're now an expert on this week's words? Then wait no longer!

1. There is an expectation that oil prices will _____ next year.

2. "Without government support, our industry will _____," warned the hotelier.

3. A steady decline in profits has forced the company to _____.

4. Over the years, the talented tailor's eyesight began to _____.

5. "That sweater might _____ if washed in warm water," warned Darius.

6. By the fifth century, the Roman Empire's power was clearly starting to _____.

7. Continued poaching will _____ some species unless action is taken now.

8. Fascinated, Will watched the hawk _____ from the sky like a stone.

9. As local supplies _____, we will be forced to import far more.

10. After hours of raging, the storm finally began to _____.

11. Hearing her mother's footsteps _____, Aki retrieved her phone from her bag.

12. "I refuse to let this debate _____ into a slanging match," said Omar flatly.

13. Recent restrictions have forced people to _____ a range of cultural events.

14. "The value of these stocks is about to _____," predicted the financial advisor.

15. A good project manager knows when to _____ responsibility to others.

16. As his popularity began to _____, the actor became increasingly reclusive.

17. The king was forced to _____ the currency to finance his costly campaign.

18. Wickets began to _____ as soon as the star bowler came on to the field.

19. When hot, metals expand; when cold, they _____.

20. As Harvey's speech dragged on, people's attention began to _____.

**How well did you do?   Total Score: _____ / 20**

# #31 Silent, but Deadly

## A. About these words...

What the **mixture** of words this week have in common is that they **all** contain **at least one sneaky silent letter** somewhere!

## B. Headcount...

Read all of this week's words carefully, then decide how many of them

You **definitely know**: _____

You **haven't seen before**: _____

You **sort of know**: _____

## C. The Top 5...

Before you start learning these words, copy out the **five** you think will be the **least useful** to you in your writing:

_____

_____

_____

_____

_____

Why do you think you won't need to use these five words?

## VOCABULARY BUILDER

This list includes several sets of related words:

- **Mind-related words:** mnemonic | psychedelic
- **Weapons-related words:** ricochet | scimitar

Can you think of any more? *(Clue: the body)*

## BRILLIANT BREAKDOWNS

**nascent:** n•as•cent

**phlegm:** ph•leg•m

**resuscitate:** res•us•c•it•ate

## This Week's Target Words!

| | |
|---|---|
| ascetic | rescind |
| czar | resuscitate |
| ensign | ricochet |
| jostle | scenic |
| knick-knack | scimitar |
| mnemonic | sepulchre |
| nascent | succumb |
| phlegm | thumbscrew |
| psychedelic | whorl |
| rapport | writhe |

## D. Notable Mnemonic...

**M-N-E-M-O-N-I-C**

**M**any **n**ice **e**lves **m**agicked **O**livia's **n**ettles **i**nto **c**arnations.

## CHEAT MODE!

**Only one** word here contains a **silent 'm'**:

**m**nemonic

**Bonus:** it also happens to be the only word in the list that **begins with 'm'**.

## POWER SPELLER'S TIPS

(i) The word **czar** can also be correctly spelt **tsar** *OR* **tzar**.

(ii) The word **knick-knack** can also be correctly spelt **nick-nack**.

## EASILY CONFUSED SPELLINGS...

**ascetic** (characterized by severe self-discipline)
**aesthetic** (relating to the appreciation of beauty)

## CAN YOU THINK OF...

A homophone for **whorl**?

## WORD NERD FACT

The verb **jostle** derives from the word *joust*, which comes from the French *jouster*, which, in turn, comes from the Latin *juxta* (near).

# TEST #31: Feeling confident you've learnt this week's words? Then give this test a go!

1. Every ship is expected to fly an _____: a flag that indicates nationality.

2. Within moments of swallowing the poison, the monkey began to _____ in agony.

3. All we know about the origin of '_____' is that it comes from 18th-century French.

4. I'm not sure how I feel about the _____ space tourism industry.

5. During the Renaissance, the _____ was a favoured instrument of torture.

6. Chelsea has shocked everyone in the office by coming to work in a _____ T-shirt.

7. "There is no reason for the parties to _____ their agreement," averred the lawyer.

8. "Ugh! I hate it when a cold moves into the _____ phase," coughed Jeff.

9. The artist's spiral patterns are inspired by a _____ of one of his own fingerprints.

10. Key to the band's success has been the great _____ between its members.

11. Every evening, tired commuters _____ for space on crowded trains.

12. "Sorry, we're late!" apologised Trish. "We just HAD to take the _____ route."

13. Logan was finding it hard not to _____ to the temptation of a second burger.

14. Nowadays, a _____ is a person appointed by the government as a policy advisor.

15. Among the artefacts discovered in the vault was an exquisitely tooled _____.

16. How often do you use a _____ to remember something important?

17. Gregory's tastes are so modest that you could call them '_____'.

18. Upon his death, Prince Talbot's body was interred in the royal _____.

19. Maria's cluttered bookshelves are home to every imaginable type of _____.

20. Thankfully, the paramedic managed to _____ the young man.

## How well did you do?   Total Score: _____ / 20

# #32 It's Gone Viral

## This Week's Target Words!

| | |
|---|---|
| algorithm | favourite |
| analytics | filter |
| archiving | geotag |
| avatar | hashtag |
| Bitmoji | impressions |
| clickbait | influencer |
| crowdsourcing | live stream |
| dashboard | metric |
| emoji | notification |
| engagement | repost |

## CHEAT MODES!

(i) The **one word** with a **'y'** is **tricky** as it **sounds like an 'i'**:

analytics

(ii) **Four** of the five **compound words** in the list are always written as **single words:**

clickbait | crowdsourcing
dashboard | hashtag

## POWER SPELLER'S TIPS

(i) While **live stream** is generally regarded as **a noun and a verb**, both forms have at least two correct spellings:

live stream OR livestream *(noun)*

live-stream OR livestream *(verb)*

(ii) **Repost** can be used as either a noun or a verb. In either case, though, it **does not need a hyphen**.

## BRILLIANT BREAKDOWN

**notification:** not•if•i•cat•ion

## DID YOU KNOW THAT...

A **dashboard** was originally a board used to protect the driver of a horse-drawn coach from mud splashes?

## A. About these words...

All the words in the list this week are ones that are now inextricable from the **seemingly inescapable world of social media**.

## B. Headcount...

Read all of this week's words carefully, then decide how many of them

You **often use**: _____

You **never use**: _____

You **sometimes use**: _____

## C. The Top 5...

Before you start learning these words, copy out the **five** that you find the **most fun**:

_____

_____

_____

_____

_____

Why do you think these are the five words that you enjoy the most?

## VOCABULARY BUILDER

Predictably, there are at least two fairly large groups of related words here:

- **Interaction-related words:** crowdsourcing | engagement | repost
- **Data-related words:** algorithm | dashboard | metric

Can you see any more words in your list that belong to either of these groups?

## USE THE RIGHT WORDS!

**Bitmoji** (a brand name for a cartoon image intended to represent and look like you)
**emoji** (a small icon, image, or symbol used to convey information)
**emoticon** (a group of keyboard characters used to represent an emotion such as :-))

# TEST #32: Find out how well you remember this week's words!

1. "That platform's user _____ is totally useless!" complained Ivan.

2. Kevin's witty _____ won him hundreds of new followers.

3. Sometimes, it can feel like everything we do is _____-driven.

4. Sheryll spent ages arguing that becoming an _____ was a good career choice.

5. "So, which _____ should I be focusing on?" asked the manager.

6. "I disliked statistics at school. Imagine how I feel about _____!" Gina commented.

7. Adding a _____ can help make your photos more discoverable.

8. "I wanted to _____ this, but I couldn't see how to do it," grumbled Chan.

9. Marco never customizes his _____ on any of his social media accounts.

10. "On average, how many daily _____ do your posts receive?" inquired the marketer.

11. Levels of _____ with content are determined by a wide range of factors.

12. Randall had to spend several hours _____ old articles on his blog.

13. It would be nice to think people have become less susceptible to _____.

14. "Why not apply a _____ to your photo to make it pop more?" Juan suggested.

15. Using _____ to answer a question can yield some intriguing results.

16. I was thrilled that there was going to be a _____ of my favourite fashion show.

17. A defining characteristic of a _____ is that it is customisable.

18. "I HATE accidentally deleting a _____ before I've read it properly!" groaned Mia.

19. Caroline seems incapable of sending me an _____-free text message.

20. "When you _____ a video, do you also leave a comment?" inquired the pollster.

**How well did you do? Total Score: _____ / 20**

# #33 Going Without

## A. About these words...

The words in this week's list are a **mixture** of **nouns, verbs, and adjectives** that are associated with **famine and other related kinds of shortages**.

## B. Headcount...

Read all of this week's words carefully, then decide how many of them

You *sort of know*: _____

You *definitely know*: _____

You *haven't seen before*: _____

## C. The Top 5...

Before you start learning these words, copy out the **five** that you think are the **most obvious** ones to be included here:

_____

_____

_____

_____

_____

Why have you chosen these five words?

## CHEAT MODES!

(i) **Two words** are **very close** in spelling. The slight difference is **highlighted in bold below:**

**de**privation | privation

(ii) **Two** words end with the *city* sound, but are **spelt differently:**

pau**city** | spar**sity**

**TIP:** the **'s's go together** in <u>s</u>par<u>s</u>ity.

## CAN YOU THINK OF...

A homonym for **straits**?

## This Week's Target Words!

| | |
|---|---|
| aridity | meagreness |
| barrenness | paucity |
| blight | pestilence |
| catastrophe | privation |
| dearth | shortage |
| deprivation | sparsity |
| destitution | starvation |
| drought | straits |
| famished | undersupply |
| lack | want |

## D. Notable Mnemonic...

**P-A-U-C-I-T-Y**

**P**etulant **A**na **u**pset **C**ora **i**n **t**own **y**esterday.

## POWER SPELLER'S TIPS

(i) **Three** words **end** with the **letter string 'vation':**

depri**vation** | pri**vation** | star**vation**

(ii) **One** word contains a **doubled consonant** because it **ends with the suffix '-ness':**

meagrene**ss** (meagre + ne**ss**)

(iii) **One** word contains **three pairs of doubled consonants** as a result of its **base word AND the addition of the suffix '-ness':**

ba<u>rr</u>e<u>nn</u>e**ss** (ba<u>rr</u>e<u>n</u> + <u>n</u>e**ss**)

(iv) And **one** word has **a doubled consonant because its base word already contains it:**

undersu**pp**ly

## EASILY CONFUSED SPELLINGS...

**drought** (water shortage resulting from a lack of rain)
**draught** (a current of cold air)

**want** (the lack of something essential)
**wont** (a person's customary behaviour)

## USEFUL USAGE...

The noun **straits** is commonly used in the expression **in dire straits**, which is employed to refer to a situation as troubled or difficult.

# TEST #33: Think you've mastered your words for the week? If so, carry on!

1.  Due to the _____ of food, the besieged citizens were forced to surrender.

2.  Facing _____, Fiona swallowed her pride and asked her wealthy aunt for help.

3.  A '_____' is a disease that affects plants and is typically caused by bacteria or fungi.

4.  "We will find ourselves in dire _____ unless we act now," insisted Arvind.

5.  Having skipped breakfast, Katrina was _____ by lunchtime.

6.  One major challenge the early settlers had to face was the _____ of the land.

7.  Countries with a _____ of natural resources often import diverse raw materials.

8.  The _____ of many people's salaries means they enjoy few luxuries.

9.  Distressed by the number of people in _____, Selma volunteered at a local charity.

10. Sadly, significant _____ is a common feature of life in a shanty town.

11. "Sire," said the sultan's advisor gravely, "this _____ is ravaging your people."

12. The unseasonal _____ has resulted in many vital crops being lost.

13. In 2021, the global scarcity of chips led to the _____ of many consumer electronics.

14. I know I shouldn't have been surprised by the _____ of the Sahara, but I was.

15. This year's rice _____ is being blamed on insufficient rainfall.

16. The _____ of food was a major contributing factor to the expedition's failure.

17. During WWII, rationing was made inevitable by the _____ of essential food items.

18. "More and more people will face _____ if things don't change," said the campaigner.

19. "You know, a _____ of water is probably why your flowers died," commented Raja.

20. Investment in aquaculture could yet help avert a _____ in wild fisheries.

**How well did you do?  Total Score: _____ / 20**

# #34 Happy Endings III

## This Week's Target Words!

| | |
|---|---|
| analgesic | peripatetic |
| antagonistic | philharmonic |
| chimeric | problematic |
| eclectic | quadraphonic |
| elliptic | rhapsodic |
| empathetic | sardonic |
| hydraulic | soporific |
| idiosyncratic | stoic |
| kinetic | systemic |
| neurotic | therapeutic |

## CHEAT MODE!

**Only one word** here contains **doubled consonants:** elliptic.

## POWER SPELLER'S TIPS

(i) **Several adjectives** here possess **correct, alternative forms, including:**

elliptic OR elliptic**al**
chimeric OR chimeric**al**
stoic OR stoic**al**
therapeutic OR therapeutic**al**

(ii) The word **quadraphonic** can **also** be correctly spelt **quadrophonic** (i.e. with an 'o').

## USE THE RIGHT WORDS!

**empathetic** (being able to understand and share another person's feelings)
**sympathetic** (having pity for someone else's misfortunes)

**systemic** (related to a system)
**systematic** (methodical, or orderly)

## WORD NERD FACT

The adjective **sardonic** ultimately derives from the Greek word **sardonion:** a plant from Sardinia with a bitter taste which was said to cause its eater to screw up their face.

## A. About these words...

This week, the list consists of a **mixture** of words that end with the **suffix '-ic'.**

**REMEMBER:** This suffix **can form nouns or adjectives** when added to a base word.

## B. Headcount...

Read all of this week's words carefully, then decide how many of them

You **sometimes use**: _____

You **often use**: _____

You **never use**: _____

## C. The Top 5...

Before you start learning these words, copy out the **five** that you think you will find the **easiest** to remember:

_____

_____

_____

_____

_____

Why do you think these five words will be the least challenging for you to learn?

## D. Notable Mnemonic...

**P-E-R-I-P-A-T-E-T-I-C**

**P**ete **e**njoys **r**ich **i**cing **p**articularly **a**fter **t**rying **E**va's **t**amarind **i**nfused **c**akes.

## BRILLIANT BREAKDOWN

**antagonistic:** an•tag•on•is•tic

## VOCABULARY BUILDER

This list includes groups of related words:

- **Music-related words:** philharmonic | quadraphonic | rhapsodic
- **Ancient Greece-related words:** chimeric | peripatetic | stoic

Can you think of any more? *(Clue: physics)*

# TEST #34: See how many words you've got the hang of this week!

1. Often _____ towards each other, ancient Greek city states frequently went to war.

2. In view of the current rail strike, intercity travel has become _____.

3. Lorries are fitted with _____ brakes because of their reliability.

4. "I've recently taken up sketching and am finding it quite _____," Regina told me.

5. An _____ such as paracetamol can help reduce swelling.

6. Banksy's _____ style has made his works highly sought after.

7. During the 1970s, _____ sound systems were all the rage.

8. "Can't you find a word to use *other* than '_____'?" snapped Luis.

9. In mythology, a _____ creature is one formed from the parts of several animals.

10. The praise being lavished on her debut novel is nothing short of _____.

11. A whistle-blower has released evidence of the company's _____ criminal negligence.

12. '_____' is one of those adjectives to which you can further add the suffix '-al'.

13. The names of many famous orchestras contain the word '_____'.

14. Louisa marvelled at the _____ mix of antiques and modern art in the gallery.

15. "Is it true that cherries have a _____ effect and can make you sleepy?" Angie asked.

16. Overwhelmed by Jumana's _____ response, Pablo burst into tears.

17. Just because a person is _____ doesn't mean they are without feelings.

18. "Classical physics defines energy as _____ energy or potential energy," she explained.

19. With a diplomat for a mother, Luna has led quite a _____ childhood.

20. Professor Wilson's students either loved or loathed her _____ wit.

How well did you do?    Total Score: _____ / 20

# #35 A Fly in the Ointment

## A. About these words...

The list this week is made up of a **cluster** of words that all entail the **sense of 'prevention' in some way**.

**TIP:** If you're unsure what a word means, look it up in your dictionary!

## B. Headcount...

Read all of this week's words carefully, then decide how many of them

You *definitely know*: _____

You *haven't seen before*: _____

You *sort of know*: _____

## C. The Top 5...

Before you start learning these words, copy out the **five** that you find the **most interesting**:

_____

_____

_____

_____

_____

Why do you think these five words appeal to you?

## USEFUL USAGE...

The noun **brick wall** is commonly used in the expression **to hit a brick wall**, meaning 'to encounter something that prevents you from doing something'.

## CAN YOU THINK OF...

A homophone for **curb**?

## This Week's Target Words!

| | |
|---|---|
| barrier | hold-up |
| brick wall | hurdle |
| constraint | impediment |
| curb | mishap |
| deterrence | obstruction |
| drawback | restraint |
| embargo | setback |
| encumbrance | snag |
| handicap | stonewall |
| hindrance | stoppage |

## CHEAT MODES!

(i) Only **one word** this week **needs a HYPHEN**:

hold-up

(ii) **Two** compound words **end with 'wall'**:

brick **wall** | stone**wall**

(iii) **Two** other compound words **end with 'back'**:

draw**back** | set**back**

(iv) **Two** words are **very close** in spelling. The slight **differences** are **highlighted below**:

**con**straint | **re**straint

## POWER SPELLER'S TIPS

(i) The **addition of the suffix '-ance'** to **two** words results in the **loss of the penultimate 'e' in each base word**:

encumbrance = encumb**e**r + ance
hindrance = hind**e**r + ance

(ii) The word **embargo** is one of those **tricky nouns that ends in 'o'** which **needs an 'es'** to form its **plural**:

embargo (s.) ⇨ embargo**es** (pl.)

## EASILY CONFUSED SPELLINGS...

**drawback** (a disadvantage)
**draw back** (to move away from something or someone)

**hold-up** (a delay or violent robbery)
**hold up** (to stay successful or strong)

# TEST #35: Feeling certain that you know your weekly words? If so, dive right in!

1.  Notwithstanding Raj's fears, his driving test passed without _____.

2.  Attempting to convince Bob he is wrong is like talking to a _____.

3.  "Don't _____," ordered Maria. "Answer the question right now!"

4.  Julia has always found gloves an _____ when doing the washing-up.

5.  Showing great _____, Mona resisted the offer of more pasta.

6.  During the Cold War, the principle of nuclear _____ was widely debated.

7.  Selma's knee injury has proven a major _____ to her training programme.

8.  What would you say is the greatest _____ to effective communication?

9.  "As far as I can see, the only _____ will be getting Anita to agree," commented Igor.

10. Before the trial, the judge ordered an _____ on the taking of photographs in court.

11. Once children overcome their shyness, you may find they talk with less _____.

12. 'Without let or _____' is a formal way of saying 'without obstruction'.

13. Our project didn't go according to plan; in fact, we hit a _____ right at the start.

14. Campaigners fear the new laws will be an _____ to securing justice for victims.

15. Vincent has been working hard to _____ his tendency to be sarcastic.

16. "Come on, guys!" yelled Aiko impatiently. "What's the _____?"

17. "I've been told the power _____ has lasted over a week," said the reporter.

18. In some sports, a _____ is imposed on superior players to make things fairer.

19. Last week, an _____ on the track delayed our train to Leeds.

20. One _____ to buying lots of books is that you soon run out of shelf space.

How well did you do?   Total Score: _____ / 20

# #36 Say Cheese!

## This Week's Target Words!

| | |
|---|---|
| aperture | grain |
| camera obscura | high-resolution |
| camera-shy | low-resolution |
| close-up | negative |
| contact sheet | overexposure |
| darkroom | photobombing |
| digital zoom | photogenic |
| exposure | selfie |
| flashbulb | sepia |
| foreground | snapshot |

## CHEAT MODES!

(i) **Two** words are **very similar**. The **difference** between them is the **prefix 'over-'**:

exposure | **over**exposure

(ii) **Two** other words are also **very similar**. The **difference also** lies in their **prefixes**:

**high**-resolution | **low**-resolution

(**Note:** both these words **need hyphens**!)

(iii) **Two** further words here **need hyphens**:

camera**-**shy | close**-**up

## VOCABULARY BUILDER

Predictably, several words in this list can be grouped together:

- **Pre-digital photography:** contact sheet | darkroom | flashbulb
- **Digital photography:** high-resolution | low-resolution | digital zoom
- **Specific types of photographs:** close-up | selfie

Can you think of any more? *(Clue: closed compound words)*

## EASILY CONFUSED SPELLINGS...

**close-up** (an image taken at close range)
**close up** (to become smaller or blocked by something)

## A. About these words...

The words in this week's list are all ones you might come across in the **picturesque world of photography & photographs** — both digital AND analogue!

## B. Headcount...

Read all of this week's words carefully, then decide how many of them

You *never use*: _____

You *often use*: _____

You *sometimes use*: _____

## C. The Top 5...

Before you start learning these words, copy out the **five** you think you will find the **most useful** to you in your writing:

_____

_____

_____

_____

_____

How do you think using these five words will help you?

## POWER SPELLER'S TIPS

(i) **Two** words have **abbreviated forms** that are **commonly used**:

high-**res**olution ⇨ **hi-res**
low-**res**olution ⇨ **lo-res**

(ii) The **plural** of 'camera obscura' is sometimes formed by **adding an 's' to the second part**:

camera obscura ⇨ camera obscura**s**

## USEFUL USAGE...

The word **grain** is often used in the expression **to go against the grain**, meaning 'to be contrary to what is natural or normal'.

# TEST #36: Positive that you're now an expert on this week's words? Then wait no longer!

1. "So," said the detective, producing a _____, "how do you explain this?"

2. _____ screens display images in an incredible amount of detail.

3. "'_____' means an image has been in the light too long," said the instructor.

4. "I often use a _____ to review a collection of images," the photographer stated.

5. To maximise the brightness of a shot, the lens _____ should be widened.

6. "For me, _____-toned photographs conjure up the late nineteenth century," he said.

7. In Photoshop, the _____ colour can be changed using the Eyedropper tool.

8. "Isn't being a _____ celebrity a contradiction in terms?" Wanda pondered.

9. Curiously, good looks do not automatically mean a person is _____.

10. Barging into the _____, Ken let in the light and ruined Hal's photos.

11. While people might think _____ is a recent trend, it's been around for years.

12. "Applying effects to _____ images can have interesting results," observed Laila.

13. The use of _____ may compromise the quality of an image.

14. High-definition _____ images can be used to create detailed textures.

15. Hearing the _____ pop, the recluse realised his picture had just been taken.

16. As far as we know, the earliest use of the term '_____' dates to 1604.

17. Adding _____ to an image can help give it a more vintage look.

18. A _____ is an image in which the light areas appear dark, and vice versa.

19. Alonzo couldn't believe that Arla had never taken a _____.

20. The _____ of an undeveloped black and white film roll to light will ruin it.

**How well did you do?    Total Score: _____ / 20**

# #37 Stop the Presses!

## A. About these words...

This week, all the entries come from another area that is now both digital and analogue: the **non-stop world of newspapers & their production**!

## B. Headcount...

Read all of this week's entries carefully, then decide how many of them

You *sort of know*: _____

You *definitely know*: _____

You *haven't seen before*: _____

## C. The Top 5...

Before you start learning these entries, copy out the **five** that are your **least favourite**:

_____

_____

_____

_____

_____

Why don't you like these five?

## D. Notable Mnemonic...

**R-E-D-A-C-T-I-O-N**

**R**estless **e**els **d**arted **a**round **c**ausing **t**etchiness **i**n **o**verweening **n**arwhals.

## USE THE RIGHT WORDS!

**byline** (a line that names the writer(s) of a newspaper article)
**headline** (the heading of a newspaper or magazine article)
**strapline** (a caption or secondary headline in a magazine or newspaper)

**redaction** (the editing or censoring of a text)
**retraction** (the withdrawal of a statement)

## This Week's Target Words!

| | |
|---|---|
| broadsheet | layout |
| byline | misquotation |
| column | photojournalist |
| copywriter | proofreading |
| distribution | quotation |
| editorial | redaction |
| fact-checking | retraction |
| font | strapline |
| the fourth estate | tabloid |
| headline | typesetting |

## CHEAT MODES!

(i) Only **one** word this week **needs a HYPHEN**:

fact-checking

(ii) Of all the compound words in this list, only **one** is **written as separate words**:

the fourth estate

(iii) All **five** words ending with the *shun* sound conclude with the **letter string 'tion'**:

distribu**tion** | misquota**tion** quota**tion** | redac**tion** | retrac**tion**

(iv) **Two pairs** of words are **very close** in spelling. The **differences** between them are **highlighted below**:

**mis**quotation & quotation re**d**action & re**tr**action

## POWER SPELLER'S TIP

**Two adjectives** can be made from **column**:

columnar (column + ar)
columned (column + ed)

## VOCABULARY BUILDER

A lot of words here can be grouped together:

- **Compound words:** broadsheet | byline | copywriter | headline | layout | photojournalist | proofreading | strapline | typesetting

Can you think of any more compound words of your own to add to this week's list? (*Clue: look at the words already in the list!*)

# TEST #37: Feeling confident you've learnt this week's words? Then give this test a go!

1. To emphasise his point, the journalist has used a _____ from *Hamlet*.

2. Today's _____ launched a scathing attack on the government's proposed budget.

3. In the pre-digital era, _____ was a laborious, manual process.

4. The purpose of a _____ is to identify the writer of an article.

5. My editor has insisted on the _____ of several sentences in my report.

6. At the start of his career, Alexis worked in advertising as a _____.

7. As the word suggests, a '_____' communicates news stories through images.

8. "Every _____ is more depressing than the last," noted Irene dolefully.

9. Not all web editions of _____ newspapers are free to access.

10. One of the borough councillors is suing a newspaper for publishing a _____.

11. Although used interchangeably, the terms '_____' and 'typeface' are not the same.

12. I'm not sure if I like the recent changes to that paper's _____.

13. "10 pages of exclusive eyewitness accounts," promised the _____.

14. Yesterday, our local paper printed a _____ for an error in its Friday edition.

15. "In the age of the internet, _____ is ever more crucial," the academic stated.

16. One characteristic of the _____ press is celebrity gossip.

17. "I detest _____," complained Nina. "It always takes so long to do properly!"

18. For years, Mrs Sanders wrote an agony aunt _____ for a well-known magazine.

19. Newspaper reporters were first referred to as '_____' in 1843.

20. A newspaper's circulation is calculated based on its average daily _____.

**How well did you do?   Total Score: _____ / 20**

# #38 T is for Trickery

## This Week's Target Words!

artifice

chicanery

covertness

cozenage

deception

dissembling

dissimulation

double-dealing

duplicity

falsehood

fraudulence

furtiveness

guile

intrigued

machinations

mendacity

skulduggery

smokescreen

stratagem

subterfuge

## POWER SPELLER'S TIPS

The word for a person who is involved in **machinations** is a **machinator**. And, **to machinate** is what a machinator does.

## VOCABULARY BUILDER

Not surprisingly, many of this week's words can be grouped together:

- **Deceit:** deception | duplicity
- **Concealment:** covertness | dissembling | dissimulation
- **Plotting & Planning:** intrigued | machinations | stratagem | subterfuge

Can you think of any more? *(Clues: lying — cunning)*

**WARNING!** While many of these words are extremely close in meaning, they **CANNOT** all be used as synonyms. Make sure to check your dictionary before you use them!

## USE THE RIGHT WORDS!

**stratagem** (a scheme or plan to outwit another person)
**strategy** (a plan of action)
**subterfuge** (deceit employed to achieve one's aims)
**sabotage** (the deliberate destruction or damaging of something for a particular aim)

## A. About these words...

The list this week is made up of a **mixture** of words that all entail the **sense of 'trickery' in some way**.

**TIP:** If you want even more words like these, look this week's ones up in your thesaurus!

## B. Headcount...

Read all of this week's words carefully, then decide how many of them

You *often use*: _____

You *sometimes use*: _____

You *never use*: _____

## C. The Top 5...

Before you start learning these words, copy out the **five** that you are **least surprised** to find here:

_____

_____

_____

_____

_____

Why do you think these five words were most likely to be included here?

## BRILLIANT BREAKDOWNS

**cozenage:** co•zen•age
**furtiveness:** fur•t•ive•ness
**machinations:** ma•chin•at•ions
**mendacity:** men•da•city

## PRONUNCIATION PUZZLES

(i) The '**ch**' in **chicanery** is pronounced *'sh'*.

(ii) '**Cozen**' at the start of the word **cozenage** is pronounced as if it were spelt *'cousin'*.

(iii) Although the word **subterfuge** *may remind you* of the word *'subtle'*, unlike 'subtle', the '**b**' in 'su**b**terfuge' is **NOT silent**.

# TEST #38: Find out how well you remember this week's words!

1. Once their financial records were audited, the level of _____ became apparent.

2. "The _____ of this mission is central to its success," stated the general.

3. "We need a new _____ to deal with this," Zhao said decisively.

4. "All this _____ will catch up with you eventually," cautioned Tina.

5. Desperate to regain his throne, the deposed king _____ with his loyal nobles.

6. The extent of her _____ has shocked and disappointed us all.

7. Growing weary of his own _____, Mr Darcy finally admitted his feelings.

8. People have become jaded by all the recent political _____.

9. "How has our pharmacy been a _____ for money laundering?" gasped Shona.

10. "I don't believe a word," snorted Ivy. "You have been _____ the whole time."

11. With a surprising lack of _____, the salesperson highlighted the product's flaws.

12. As a child, Amira loved reading tales of pirates and their _____.

13. '_____' is a late sixteenth-century word meaning 'trickery'.

14. Identifying where truth ends and _____ begins can be complicated sometimes.

15. "Considerable _____ went into staging this hacking," observed the analyst.

16. Catalina was unimpressed by her sister's _____ to fool their parents.

17. The vizier hid his _____ well and, as such, misled many people.

18. "Be done with your _____; tell me the truth," she commanded.

19. Lucilla kicked herself for having been taken in so easily by Pete's _____.

20. "It was the _____ of his behaviour that first made me suspicious," said Kay.

How well did you do?    Total Score: _____ / 20

# #39 That's a Proper Word?!?!

## A. About these words...

Believe it or not, all the words in this week's final list are **actually proper words**...

## B. Headcount...

Read all of this week's words carefully, then decide how many of them

You **haven't seen before**: _____

You **sort of know**: _____

You **definitely know**: _____

## C. The Top 5...

Before you start learning these words, copy out the **five** that you think are the **most entertaining**:

_____

_____

_____

_____

_____

Why are these five words the most fun?

## D. Notable Mnemonic...

**F-I-L-I-B-U-S-T-E-R**

**F**ive **i**diotic **l**ions **i**n **b**alaclavas **u**sed **s**poons **t**o **e**at **r**adishes.

## USEFUL USAGES...

The noun **caboodle** is often used in the expression **the whole caboodle**, meaning 'the entirety of a thing or group of people'.

In a similar vein, the noun **shebang** is frequently used in the expression **the whole shebang**, which means 'the entirety of a thing'.

## This Week's Target Words!

| | |
|---|---|
| caboodle | mishmash |
| codswallop | murmuration |
| discombobulate | namby-pamby |
| filibuster | nincompoop |
| fisticuffs | obfuscate |
| flibbertigibbet | piffle |
| hotchpotch | shebang |
| ichor | shenanigans |
| kowtow | switcheroo |
| lugubrious | titbit |

## CHEAT MODES!

(i) **Three** words contain the **same doubled vowels**:

cab**oo**dle | nincomp**oo**p | switcher**oo**

(ii) **Four** other words contain at least one pair of **doubled consonants**:

codswa**ll**op | fisticu**ff**s
fli**bb**ertigi**bb**et | pi**ff**le

(iii) **Five** words are almost the same word twice over. The **slight differences** between each of the 'two halves' are **highlighted below**:

**h**otch**p**otch | **k**ow**t**ow
**m**ish**m**ash | **n**amby-**p**amby | **t**it**b**it

## VOCABULARY BUILDER

While this week's words are quite eclectic, there are still a few small sets here:

- **Trickery-related words:** shenanigans | switcheroo
- **Excessive speech-related words:** filibuster | flibbertigibbet

Can you think of any more? *(Clue: nonsense)*

## SYNONYM SPOTTING

Although it's quite hard to find synonym pairs in this list, there are two!

- discombobulate = obfuscate
- hotchpotch = mishmash

Can you think of any synonyms of your own for other words in your list?

## TEST #39: Think you've mastered your words for the week? If so, for the last time, carry on!

1. The latest blockbuster is a _____ of unresolved plot lines and 2D characters.

2. Tina loves Halloween: the costumes, the pumpkins, the horror films — the whole _____.

3. "Fantasy fiction? Pah!" scoffed Monique. "It's all utter _____!"

4. The word '_____' can be used as a collective noun for starlings.

5. "Gentlemen, _____ are not allowed on the premises," said the club owner sternly.

6. "Don't be such a _____!" exclaimed Fred. "Of course, we're still friends!"

7. "He never makes any sense; all he ever spouts is _____," she complained.

8. "So," Santa said to his elves, "what _____ have you been up to in my absence?"

9. "I refuse to _____ to the imposter!" declared the princess stoutly.

10. "Your lies will not _____ the truth," stated the sheriff. "I know you betrayed me."

11. A '_____' is a person who talks excessively, or who is frivolous and irresponsible.

12. "The meal was an inedible _____ of Japanese and Italian cuisines," declared Fran.

13. Falling for the old _____, Disa was conned into buying a fake designer handbag.

14. I know it's a bit unfair, but bulldogs always seem to have _____ faces.

15. "Don't be such a _____!" scolded Omar. "You didn't bash yourself *that* hard!"

16. "Your attempts to _____ me aren't working," said Paolo smugly.

17. "Ooh, look! Your cat's eyeing the last _____ on your plate," chuckled Alicia.

18. "I can't believe it," said Dido, shaking her head. "Juno is running the whole _____."

19. According to Greek mythology, _____, not blood, ran in the veins of the gods.

20. "What are you trying to do?" interrupted Rita rudely. "Stage a _____?"

### How well did you do?   Total Score: _____ / 20

# NOTES FOR PARENTS & TEACHERS

## The Spelling Tests Transcripts

On the following pages (pp. 84-103), you will find the full transcripts for the 39 spelling tests in this workbook. Each transcript consists of the 20 sentences included in its respective test, complete with the missing target spelling marked in bold. For example, if the target spelling were the word '**playground**', you would find a sentence like the one below in the test transcript:

10. The **playground** was full of laughing children.

## Suggestions for Administering the Spelling Tests

How you administer the tests is up to you, but you might find one of the following methods helpful:

**Method 1:**
- Read out the sentence along with the missing word, saying aloud: *The playground was full of laughing children*

**Method 2:**
- Read out the target spelling first, saying aloud: *Playground*
- Wait for a few seconds
- Then read out the whole sentence, saying aloud: *The playground was full of laughing children*

**Method 3:**
- Start with a brief statement like: *Spelling Number 10 is playground*, or *Number 10 is playground*, or *The word is playground*
- Wait for a few seconds
- Then read out the whole sentence, saying aloud: *The playground was full of laughing children*

## Suggestions for Timing & Marking the Spelling Tests

**It is entirely up to you how much time you wish to give your child to do the tests**. You may wish to remove the time factor so that they feel less anxious or pressured. Alternatively, you may want to make the spelling tests a bit of a challenge, in which case, set a time limit (e.g. 15 minutes) that you feel is appropriate for your child.

Each test carries **a maximum of 20 marks**. However, **how to award marks is also left to your discretion**. You may wish to award 1 mark for each correct answer and 0 marks for any incorrect answers. Alternatively, to encourage your child, you might want to award half marks in some instances; for example, when a word is spelt correctly, but is missing a necessary capital letter.

## GOOD LUCK!

# SPELLING TESTS TRANSCRIPTS

### Term 1: Test 1

1 | Until 1916, certain items such as rubber, cotton, and soap were deemed **contraband**.
2 | Following the **assassination** of Archduke Franz Ferdinand, war was inevitable in 1914.
3 | Various tactical challenges during WWI lead to a revolution in **infantry** techniques.
4 | Siegfried Sassoon's poem "**Counter-Attack**" vividly depicts the experience of trench warfare.
5 | In 1917, the US government began to **draft** men into the armed forces.
6 | Relentlessly, German **U-boat** wolf packs stalked their prey off the Irish coast.
7 | With the outbreak of war, Britain's **propaganda** machine went into overdrive.
8 | After Germany violated Belgian neutrality, the **Allies** quickly deployed their troops.
9 | The philosopher Bertrand Russell was a **pacifist** who refused to fight.
10 | Although part of the Triple **Entente**, Britain was reluctant to join the war.
11 | Women working in the **munitions** factories played a crucial role in the war effort.
12 | '**Doughboy**' was a nickname for a particular type of American soldier during WWI.
13 | In November 1918, an **armistice**, rather than a surrender, finally ended the carnage.
14 | The creation of a **convoy** system reduced German attacks on Allied shipping.
15 | **Dreadnought** battleships were among the many craft that fought in the Battle of Jutland.
16 | Men going "over the top" stood little chance against the enemy's **machine guns**.
17 | The 1916 imposition of **conscription** gave rise to demonstrations in Trafalgar Square.
18 | As a result of a **land mine** explosion, several soldiers were killed.
19 | Following intensive negotiations, a multilateral **treaty** was finally ratified in 1919.
20 | Flying too low, the French reconnaissance aircraft were hit by **artillery** fire.

### Term 1: Test 2

1 | Scholarly research has shown there is often a **kernel** of truth in many legends.
2 | A near-fatal experience may prompt even an **atheist** to turn to some form of faith.
3 | To escape the unexpected downpour, we sheltered in a covered **pavilion**.
4 | "Guerrillas continue to **harass** the army in the mountains," noted the commentator.
5 | Realising he'd been outmanoeuvred, the general was forced to **concede** defeat.
6 | Liam's **outrageous** suggestion shocked everyone at the meeting.
7 | To prevent the contagious disease spreading, patients were placed in **quarantine**.
8 | A team of vets has been assigned to **inoculate** all the cattle in the herd.
9 | "Sales of electric cars will **supersede** those of petrol models in five years," predicted Ian.
10 | Faced with a serious **dilemma**, Ethan asked his father for advice.
11 | Only authorised **personnel** are allowed access to the bank's vault.
12 | "I guarantee that a ride on that roller coaster will **exhilarate** you!" enthused Selma.
13 | Lacking sufficient proof, the police couldn't **indict** the suspect.
14 | The company has apologised for the **omission** of key information on its website.
15 | A boom in bridge-building all over the world marked the **millennium**.
16 | Mimicking its habitat, the Solomon Island frog's skin provides it with superb **camouflage**.
17 | After months of **perseverance**, the journalist tracked down the missing whistle-blower.
18 | Edward Lear's *Book of Nonsense* is full of **humorous** limericks and illustrations.
19 | To better **gauge** public opinion, the government will hold a referendum.
20 | The pianist was as famous for her **idiosyncrasy** of performing barefoot as for her playing.

## Term 1: Test 3

1. Finding the new play too **pedestrian**, the audience quickly became restless.
2. Thankfully, apart from hitting a bit of turbulence, our flight was **uneventful**.
3. "Don't be put off by the book's **drab** cover — it's fascinating!" enthused Archie.
4. Without plenty of seasoning, you'll find that potato and leek soup **insipid**.
5. Although Gordon's administrative job is **tedious**, the pay is good.
6. Except for the odd weekend away, the lawyer led a very **prosaic** life.
7. "Cole's suggestions are always **vapid**; they're never exciting," she warned.
8. The architect's designs were rejected by the client as being too **unimaginative**.
9. We were disappointed to discover that the new sitcom was incredibly **stodgy**.
10. Though that song has a catchy rhythm, its **banal** lyrics let it down.
11. Reorganising your schedule is one solution to a **monotonous** routine.
12. As Uncle Tony is allergic to most spices, his food is unavoidably **bland**.
13. Despite all the hype, the latest superhero movie couldn't be more **unsensational**.
14. The match was decidedly **boring**: neither side scored a single goal.
15. "A solid, but **unspectacular** performance," read a two-star review of the concert.
16. I'm not fond of landscape paintings; I often find them **dreary** and uninvolving.
17. For years, Professor Green's students have dreaded his **ponderous** philosophy lectures.
18. To escape his **humdrum** existence, Lorenzo decided to travel the world.
19. The characterizations in this new novel are quite **stale**; they all feel overfamiliar.
20. With its flat fields and marshes, the surrounding countryside was quite **undramatic**.

## Term 1: Test 4

1. The police are considering the possibility that a **terrorist** caused the explosion.
2. Bugs Bunny is by far my favourite cartoon **confidence trickster**.
3. Evidence suggests an **arsonist** was responsible for the forest blaze.
4. According to our family legends, one of our ancestors was a tea **smuggler**.
5. The **hijacker** terrified the passengers by threatening to blow up their plane.
6. "The ghost of a hanged **poacher** haunts these woods," whispered the gamekeeper.
7. Monique loves watching old **gangster** movies on a rainy Sunday afternoon.
8. In Renaissance England, a **pickpocket** was sometimes referred to as a 'cutpurse'.
9. To release the politician's child, the **kidnapper** demanded five million pounds in ransom.
10. The **vandal** responsible for slashing the *Mona Lisa* remains unidentified.
11. The focus of a nationwide manhunt, the **abductor** decided to turn himself in.
12. Ned Kelly, the infamous Australian bushranger, was a convicted police **murderer**.
13. After years of stealing funds from his employer, the **embezzler** was finally caught.
14. Yesterday, the president was gunned down by a masked **assassin**.
15. "Any **trespasser** found on this property will be prosecuted," read the sign.
16. Interpol have finally arrested that notorious drug **trafficker**.
17. Using a stolen identity, the **fraudster** avoided paying taxes for years.
18. The rise of the mobile phone has created a new type of criminal: the **phone hacker**.
19. Deploying viruses or phishing are two offences a **cybercriminal** might commit.
20. Jo was charged with being an **abettor** for helping Mike with his scamming operation.

**Term 1: Test 5**

1  Mr Chan stood at the door beaming with **benevolence** as his guests arrived.

2  The glorious spring sunshine was a **benison** after endless winter skies.

3  In *Great Expectations*, Pip mistakenly believes Miss Havisham is his **benefactress**.

4  Judging from the **malodorous** smell of the bins, food was rotting inside them.

5  As her father's only child, Chloe was the sole **beneficiary** of his billions.

6  With a look of unalloyed **malice**, the sorcerer disappeared in a puff of smoke.

7  A well-known literary critic's **benediction** can impact massively on a book's sales.

8  The donation of a generous **benefactor** has saved our local museum from closure.

9  With the factory explosion came the release of **malignant** chemical fumes.

10  Paolo finds being bilingual **beneficial** in all sorts of surprising ways.

11  It took the words of just one **malcontent** to stir the crowd to rebellion.

12  Examining the company's records has revealed ample proof of **malfeasance**.

13  Before the knights went off to war, Friar Francis said a short **benedictory** prayer.

14  "Sadly, there's no quick fix to our economic **malaise**," admitted the chancellor.

15  In revenge, the spiteful warlock invoked a **malediction** on the entire kingdom.

16  The remote village was struck down by an unknown **malady**; no one survived.

17  That the accused was a **malefactor** of the highest order was borne out by the evidence.

18  Our previous mayor is fondly remembered for her numerous acts of **beneficence**.

19  Children are among those most likely to suffer from **malnutrition** in war-torn countries.

20  His **benign** appearance completely belied the fact that he was a killer.

**Term 1: Test 6**

1  When the inmates' privileges were revoked, a **riot** broke out in the prison.

2  The courtroom descended into **bedlam** at the jury's verdict of not guilty.

3  Incensed protesters have gone on the **rampage** and are damaging property.

4  "This tropical storm is wreaking indescribable **havoc**," said the reporter solemnly.

5  Last week, a heated debate in our history lesson ended in **uproar**.

6  The **pandemonium** caused by a rat at Lady Delaware's luncheon is now legendary.

7  Disturbed by a **commotion** outside, Amit went to investigate.

8  Rosa's surprise party at the weekend was a complete **fiasco**.

9  The board has been in **turmoil** since the company's disgraced director resigned.

10  Burglars ransacked our home, leaving it in complete **disarray**.

11  "Widespread civil **unrest** will follow if this law is passed," predicted the analyst.

12  After twenty years of brutal **misrule**, the dictator was eventually overthrown.

13  **Anarchy** reigned in France following the storming of the Bastille in 1789.

14  Anita stared helplessly at the **chaos** of her teenage daughter's room.

15  To prevent further **misorder** in the streets, the army has been called in.

16  A **furore** has erupted owing to the proposed closure of our local primary school.

17  Famously, the premiere of Igor Stravinsky's ballet *The Rite of Spring* ended in **mayhem**.

18  The *Beagle*'s captain successfully steered her through the seething **maelstrom**.

19  Britain witnessed great social **disorder** just after the end of the Napoleonic Wars.

20  Powerless to quell the **tumult**, the emperor ordered the massacre of his citizens.

## Term 1: Test 7

1. "Now we've met, I realise my **preconception** of you was all wrong," admitted Freya.
2. "This groundbreaking project calls for a **brainstorm**," the team leader declared.
3. To test her **hypothesis**, the scientist performed a series of experiments.
4. The jury took very little time to arrive at the **conclusion** that the witness was lying.
5. Children's experiences and social interactions help develop their **cognition**.
6. The professor sheepishly confessed that his thesis was not actually his **brainchild**.
7. "No great discovery was ever made without a bold **guess**," he quipped.
8. About to give up in despair, Ned had a sudden **brainwave**.
9. Ezra's **hunch** that Sugarplum would win the steeplechase proved very lucrative.
10. "Talking about this problem in **abstraction** won't solve it," grumbled Jorge.
11. Bert's **supposition** that I could help him could not have been more wrong.
12. "Without facts," retorted Mr Gradgrind, "you have nothing but **conjecture**."
13. Ivan spent hours trying to explain the **concept** of quantum mechanics to me.
14. "Holmes, you truly are a master of **deduction**," marvelled Dr Watson.
15. Your five senses help shape your **perception** of the world around you.
16. **Inspiration** is often found in the most unlikely of places.
17. As a precaution, the doctor kept Maisie in hospital overnight under **observation**.
18. It only took Karl a matter of minutes to grasp Einstein's **theory** of relativity.
19. The committee's report was useless as it was largely based on **speculation**.
20. "You have absolutely no **conception** of responsibility!" Ricky's mother scolded.

## Term 1: Test 8

1. *The Merriam-Webster Dictionary* dates the first known use of '**intelligentsia**' to 1905.
2. Being **malleable** metals, lead and silver are easily hammered into shapes.
3. The **intermittency** of wind and sunshine could adversely affect our electricity supply.
4. Scholars believe that the practice of **bloodletting** began with the ancient Egyptians.
5. During Queen Elizabeth I's long reign, numerous plots to **assassinate** her were foiled.
6. **Surreptitiously**, Fernando glanced about him before pocketing the gold necklace.
7. Plans are well underway to **commercialise** this latest scientific discovery.
8. "Your **embellishment** of the truth is not helping you," the headmistress warned sternly.
9. Much more must be done to **attenuate** the devastating impact of extreme weather.
10. We encourage students to participate in **extracurricular** activities to broaden their horizons.
11. "I have no idea whether that figure was real or just a **hallucination**," he confessed.
12. In certain kinds of books, the **quintessential** hero is tall, dark, and handsome.
13. Gigi learned that the **allocation** of tickets was on a first-come, first-served basis.
14. "She is a **consummate** liar. Never, ever trust her!" hissed Ahmed.
15. Falling on the shed's **corrugated** roof, the hailstones beat out a thudding tattoo.
16. "To **apportion** blame at this stage is pointless," Titus advised.
17. Being a **connoisseur** of coffee, Uncle Jo can talk for hours on the subject.
18. Guaranteed to laugh at the most **inopportune** moments, my cousin is a social liability.
19. Magnanimously, King Arthur granted the **supplicant** sanctuary in Camelot.
20. It has been frequently observed that most people's faces are **asymmetric**.

## Term 1: Test 9

1. The young officer soon found that **decoding** intercepts was a painstaking job.
2. Having an **insider** in the Persian camp ensured the Athenians' ultimate victory.
3. When his false identity was compromised, the agent fled to the nearest **safe house**.
4. Julius Caesar used a form of **encryption** to convey secret messages to his generals.
5. The **interception** of hostile aircraft was greatly facilitated by fitting radar sets into planes.
6. "**Counter-Intelligence** Officers Uncover London Spy Ring!" screamed the headlines.
7. The Enigma machine is among the most famous **cipher** devices in recent history.
8. A series of arrests convinced the group that they had been infiltrated by a **mole**.
9. In wartime, acts of **sabotage** are most likely to be ascribed to enemy agents.
10. To this day, **counter-espionage** is a priority for many countries.
11. The advent of drones has revolutionised how **reconnaissance** is carried out.
12. **Counterfeiting** documents occurs in a shockingly large number of settings.
13. Some forms of **interrogation** are no longer used, having been classified as torture.
14. For many people, leaking secret documents to the media is an act of **espionage**.
15. "What do you know about the **recruitment** of spies during the Cold War?" Vikram asked.
16. Slowly but surely, everyone was drawn into the spy's web of **deceit**.
17. Close inspection proved the driver's passport to be a **forgery**.
18. Another term that is used to refer to a **handler** is 'case officer'.
19. A fascinating, new history of the **Secret Service** has just been published.
20. The possible evidence of **cryptography** in an ancient Egyptian tomb remains disputed.

## Term 1: Test 10

1. With no money to pay her debts, the entrepreneur had to declare herself **bankrupt**.
2. The hit TV series, *Downton Abbey*, follows the lives of a **moneyed** English family.
3. Once they reach a certain threshold, **prospering** businesses often invest in expansion.
4. The firm has been declared **insolvent** following its inability to repay its loans.
5. The Wall Street Crash of 1929 left innumerable families in **straitened** circumstances.
6. "Our **pauperised** communities must be our top priority," declared the minister.
7. **Cash-strapped** or not, savvy shoppers are on the constant look-out for bargains.
8. If Pierre is feeling **flush**, he treats himself to an expensive dinner.
9. Upon her death, the film star was **impecunious**, despite earning a fortune in her heyday.
10. Karl Marx believed that the masses were exploited by the **privileged** few.
11. After decades of mismanagement, the country's **beggared** economy finally collapsed.
12. When they could not pay their rent, the **indigent** tenants were evicted.
13. Across the world, many **poverty-stricken** communities struggle to make ends meet.
14. Though sometimes **necessitous**, Ronaldo is happy in his chosen life as an artist.
15. Measures are being taken to stimulate business in economically **distressed** areas.
16. "I believe **well-to-do** citizens have an obligation to help others," she said stoutly.
17. Despite being a successful poet and playwright, Oscar Wilde died **penniless** in Paris.
18. Welfare systems are designed to help support **underprivileged** members of societies.
19. "She may not look like it," Jan whispered, "but, actually, that woman is **loaded**."
20. The less **affluent** Romans, known as plebeians, struggled to gain political equality.

## Term 1: Test 11

1. Luckily, the family possessed the documents proving their **ownership** of the property.
2. We all agree that Karim has the **leadership** skills necessary for this role.
3. More **censorship** laws to muzzle the press are being proposed.
4. After ten years of working together, the brothers dissolved their **partnership**.
5. **Internship** programmes are often run by large companies and non-profit organisations.
6. *The **Fellowship** of the Ring* is the first volume of J. R. R. Tolkien's epic fantasy trilogy.
7. "Real political **bipartisanship** entails both parties working together," observed Seth.
8. "Remember, the bonds of sibling **kinship** are sacred," the guru instructed.
9. My cousin Maria was overjoyed when she won a **scholarship** to go to film school.
10. I stood in the ruins of the Roman villa, speechless at the **workmanship** in the mosaics.
11. Anton's brother has been offered a research **assistantship** at a famous laboratory.
12. Whether fairly or not, doctors have long been reputed to have poor **penmanship** skills.
13. To boost its **readership**, that magazine is now offering reduced subscriptions.
14. "Do what you want!" Luc snapped. "This isn't a **dictatorship**!"
15. Blake set up his own business having served his **apprenticeship** as a plumber.
16. Although the group's act was undeniably polished, it needed more **showmanship**.
17. The president's **premiership** was tarnished by allegations of nepotism.
18. Famously, Hever Castle was the scene of Anne Boleyn and Henry VIII's **courtship**.
19. Machiavelli's treatise for rulers on **statesmanship**, *The Prince*, remains a controversial work.
20. Stephen Hawking's **professorship** at Cambridge was once held by Sir Isaac Newton.

## Term 1: Test 12

1. The smell of sausages sizzling **enticingly** in the kitchen greeted a ravenous Ben.
2. The prisoner's attempted escape was **thwarted** by an enterprising guard.
3. Smiling **charismatically** at the cameras, the celebrity waved once and was gone.
4. With Ariadne's assistance, Theseus' **audacious** plan to kill the Minotaur succeeded.
5. **Deliriously** happy with her results, Mona called her parents immediately.
6. Acting under orders, the knights turned the peasants' protest into a **bloodbath**.
7. The slow-swinging pendulum had a seemingly **hypnotic** effect on Ricardo.
8. Tempting the children with her gingerbread house, the **insidious** witch beckoned.
9. At the end of a **riveting** performance of *War Horse*, the audience cheered wildly.
10. For years, people believed that a nuclear **Armageddon** was an inevitability.
11. Tourists are always **beguiled** by the history-laden atmosphere of our ancient city.
12. On such a hot summer's day, the ice-cold mountain lake was an **alluring** prospect.
13. We gazed on in awe as the figure skaters glided **effortlessly** across the ice.
14. Amidst the clouds of tear gas, the protesters **defiantly** refused to move.
15. Try as she might, Miranda couldn't **vanquish** her overwhelming fear of spiders.
16. "To free the **beauteous** maiden, the warlock must be slain," the fairy told Sir Balin.
17. "Our enemy's day of **reckoning** will come!" the defeated chieftain vowed to his men.
18. Jason's **flawless** dives earned him a gold medal at the Olympics.
19. "If you *will* **tantalise** the cat, expect it to scratch you," Rahim told his sister.
20. As night set in, a sense of impending **doom** descended over the besieged city.

## Term 1: Test 13

1 | "Today's meeting was, **in sum**, an unmitigated disaster," grumbled Gerald.
2 | "**On the whole**, I believe this project should go ahead," the mayor declared.
3 | Our lawyer admitted to being **wholly** unprepared for the judge's ruling.
4 | Her early poems deal with death; **comparatively**, her later works focus on love.
5 | "Unfortunately, **in practice**, this approach will be too time-consuming," noted Varsha.
6 | The Romantic poets Byron, Keats, and Shelley valued feelings **above all** else.
7 | Serious repercussions will **undoubtedly** follow the prime minister's latest announcement.
8 | The critics called the book a triumph and the public seemed to think **likewise**.
9 | "**In short**," said Ali's instructor bluntly, "you must work much harder."
10 | The collector was determined to purchase the portrait **regardless** of cost.
11 | Punctuality is a desirable trait; **by the same token**, meticulousness is sought after.
12 | "There is a rehearsal tomorrow, **insofar as** I am aware," stated Oliver.
13 | "**On balance**, I don't think anyone has benefited from this," said Marina wisely.
14 | The cuckoo is unusual **inasmuch as** the female lays her eggs in other birds' nests.
15 | "I'm no expert, **admittedly**; but I do know that that *isn't* linguine," sniffed Sita.
16 | The disgraced head of the committee resigned **lest** he be fired.
17 | Currently, we have a glut of strawberries; **conversely**, raspberries are scarce.
18 | Two candidates happened to have the same name; **hence** the confusion.
19 | "It's a good plan **in theory**, but it needs to be costed," Ashish observed.
20 | **All told**, the article fails to make a persuasive argument.

## Term 2: Test 14

1 | When you observe something rotating, you are witnessing the effect of **centripetal force**.
2 | A conductor's **resistance** is affected by the material from which it is made.
3 | The term '**diffraction**' can be used in relation to both sound waves and light waves.
4 | In nuclear physics, '**half-life**' describes the speed of radioactive decay.
5 | The first atoms of **antimatter** were created in 1995 by physicists working at CERN.
6 | Apparently, microwave ovens use the same **frequency** band as Wi-Fi networks!
7 | Varying wavelengths each undergo a different **refraction** upon entering a glass prism.
8 | A clear example of **diffusion** is the spread of perfume in the still air of a room.
9 | The early televisions developed by John Logie Baird depended on **cathode rays**.
10 | Simply put, a **decibel** is the unit used for measuring the loudness of sound.
11 | The closer an object's **centre of gravity** is to the ground, the more stable it is.
12 | Like many measurements, the **joule** is named after a famous physicist.
13 | If your electronic device is powered by a battery, it will use **direct current**.
14 | "I've forgotten the difference between a volt and an **ampere**!" groaned Silas.
15 | Within the International System of Units, 'N' is the symbol for '**newton**'.
16 | While first used in optics, the term '**spectrum**' is now widely used in other contexts.
17 | Did you know that **centrifugal force** is defined as an apparent, rather than an actual, force?
18 | Generally speaking, a **diode** conducts an electric current in one direction.
19 | In the average household, appliances such as fridges run on an **alternating current**.
20 | One way heat can be transferred is through **convection**.

**Term 2: Test 15**

1   The disclosure of the minister's **hypocrisy** has made his position untenable.
2   "Briony is **hypersensitive** to criticism," Barry warned. "She doesn't take it well."
3   "One possible **hyponym** of 'vegetable' is 'turnip'," explained Miss Jasper.
4   If you are **hypertensive**, you should monitor your salt intake.
5   As Angela is **hypoglycaemic**, she always carries something sugary with her.
6   "Clicking on that **hyperlink** will take you to the website you need," Mo told Ivy.
7   On the night the *Titanic* sank, many of its passengers tragically died of **hypothermia**.
8   "I have no idea what a **hyperbola** is," admitted Jan.
9   Malcolm, who is **hypotensive**, suffers from abnormally low blood pressure.
10  Being **hyperactive**, Naomi often finds it difficult to concentrate.
11  To avoid triggering an adverse reaction, use detergents marked '**hypoallergenic**'.
12  **Hyperacidity** can be caused by eating spicy food.
13  People with **hypochondria** are given to diagnosing themselves with imaginary ailments.
14  '**Hypotaxis**' is a literary term that describes how clauses relate to their sentences.
15  Severe heatstroke can lead to **hyperthermia** in some cases.
16  Rihanna cringed as the nurse picked up a large **hypodermic** needle.
17  Many ads use **hyperbolic** language to exaggerate the benefits of products.
18  "You're so **hypocritical**! You say one thing and then do the opposite," snapped Fred.
19  Not wanting to be **hypercritical**, I only pointed out one problem with her plan.
20  **Hypertext** enables extensive cross-referencing both within and beyond a single text.

**Term 2: Test 16**

1   Karl regarded being fired as a **heaven-sent** opportunity to change his career.
2   The mage was tasked with identifying a **propitious** day for the king's coronation.
3   It was purely **coincidental** that we met at the train station that morning.
4   Jacinda waited patiently for an **opportune** moment to raise the issue.
5   The **calamitous** defeat of the duke's forces left the city undefended.
6   "It was just **fluky** that I won," Claudia insisted modestly.
7   The adjective '**star-crossed**' is now inextricably linked to Romeo and Juliet.
8   Glancing at the **ominous** black clouds overhead, Delia picked up her pace.
9   Lured by the sirens' song, the **hapless** sailor leapt into the sea.
10  A combination of **fortuitous** circumstances led to Jake's promotion.
11  After he was robbed for a third time, Niko began to believe he was **jinxed**.
12  In 1616, Sir Walter Raleigh set off on his **ill-starred** venture to find El Dorado.
13  In hindsight, it seemed **providential** that they had left the day before the snowstorm.
14  Owing to an **infelicitous** similarity of names, Pierre was mistakenly arrested.
15  Many **luckless** climbers have failed to conquer Mount Everest.
16  Subsequent events would prove Bernard's choice of business partner **felicitous**.
17  A **serendipitous** discovery is one that is made by happy coincidence.
18  "I believe in **karmic** justice; what goes around, comes around," declared Lola.
19  With such formidable talent, Marcus was clearly **destined** to succeed.
20  "Leave this **accursed** town," the lad urged. "You will not survive the night."

## Term 2: Test 17

1. The defence team have summoned an **expert witness** to testify tomorrow.
2. "The coroner is expected to record a **verdict** of death by misadventure," stated Elias.
3. Unsurprisingly, the leaders of the coup were given life **imprisonment**.
4. In Britain, minor cases are presided over by a **magistrate**, not a judge.
5. An impartial **arbitrator** was called in to settle the companies' dispute.
6. Through lack of evidence, the **prosecutor** has had to drop all the charges.
7. The judge reminded the **jury** not to discuss the case outside the court.
8. "Will we be able to secure a **conviction** with this?" queried the detective.
9. "I believe community service is preferable to **incarceration**," opined the judge.
10. The **plaintiff** should have been awarded significant damages, but she wasn't.
11. "The importance of the presumption of **innocence** cannot be overstated," he declared.
12. One of the duties of a **bailiff** is to serve court documents.
13. Many of the accounts that were heard in court last week were **hearsay**.
14. Having been a **litigator** for thirty years, Amit decided it was time to retire.
15. Despite her refusal to admit her **guilt**, the police have a strong case against her.
16. In some countries, a lawyer is more commonly called an **advocate**.
17. Calls are growing for the country's **justice** system to be overhauled.
18. We were all shocked by the severity of Dan's **sentence**.
19. The hearing has been postponed as the **defendant** is too ill to attend.
20. "This **accusation** of embezzlement is utter nonsense!" fumed the manager.

## Term 2: Test 18

1. Having lost, the defending champion had a decidedly disgruntled **mien**.
2. While they look similar, tangerines and clementines are two **discrete** fruits.
3. Students are expected to **cite** evidence from multiple sources in their essays.
4. The store's closing-down sale attracted a **horde** of bargain hunters.
5. As the incense in the **censer** began to burn, a gentle fragrance filled the air.
6. Using an **auger**, the carpenter bored two holes in the piece of wood.
7. The young **fawn** stayed close to its mother, eyeing the rabbit curiously.
8. In the Middle Ages, artisans of the same craft would often form a **guild** together.
9. My Aunt Nini is an avid consumer of political **satire**.
10. The **hoard** of treasure found at Sutton Hoo was the discovery of a lifetime.
11. Prior to publication, the **censor** removed certain paragraphs from the novel.
12. "Wendy's so **mean**! She won't return my scooter," wailed Tina.
13. The proposed **site** of a new nuclear power station is being hotly disputed.
14. Climbing ever higher, the sun's rays seemed to **gild** the distant mountain tops.
15. "Mr Tumnus" is the name of the **faun** in *The Lion, The Witch and The Wardrobe*.
16. Hovering above us, the whirring of the helicopter's **rotor** blades was deafening.
17. "Your cousin is incapable of being **discreet**; he's an awful gossip," complained Eric.
18. "I fear these events do not **augur** well," she noted darkly.
19. According to the new **rota**, Nurse Maggie is on night duty this week.
20. A **satyr** is a mythological being which is half-man and half-goat.

**Term 2: Test 19**

1   Staring at his spitting image, Fabio realised he'd just met his **doppelgänger**.

2   Did you know that **Neanderthal** man was actually very intelligent and accomplished?

3   Our local **delicatessen** always stocks a wide range of imported cheeses.

4   When the class bully was finally punished, several children felt a sense of **schadenfreude**.

5   "You shouldn't **angst** so much; it isn't good for you," advised Lauren.

6   Poor Igor cracked a tooth while eating a bowl of **muesli** for breakfast.

7   Consumed by **wanderlust**, the two friends spent a year travelling across Asia.

8   In a literary work, a **leitmotif** can sometimes be difficult to distinguish from a symbol.

9   In 1940, Germany launched a devastating **blitzkrieg** against the United Kingdom.

10   One of the **Bauhaus** movement's aims was to combine aesthetics with functionality.

11   Draped over the princess's bed was a deep red, silk-covered **eiderdown**.

12   "To escape, the prisoner had to **abseil** down that sheer cliff," the reporter noted.

13   Having once choked badly on a **pretzel**, Lucille never eats them now.

14   "This poster perfectly captures the **zeitgeist** of 1960s Italy," stated the art historian.

15   In 1920, a **putsch** to oust the Weimar Republic was attempted by Wolfgang Kapp.

16   Despite the salesman's enthusiastic **spiel**, the customer was unimpressed.

17   When the German tourist sneezed, I couldn't resist saying, "**Gesundheit!**"

18   Many Victorian novels were written in the hugely popular **Bildungsroman** genre.

19   "I *swear* that rattling isn't the pipes. It's a **poltergeist!**" hissed Mervat.

20   Aged only eight, Tiger Woods established himself as a golf **wunderkind**.


**Term 2: Test 20**

1   One function of a play's **prologue** is to capture the audience's initial interest.

2   Despite her advisors' anxieties, the childless queen refused to name her **successor**.

3   "Don't **postdate** those cheques; my workers need paying today," instructed the foreman.

4   In a **subsequent** search of the suspect's house, the stolen goods were found.

5   Stonehenge is among the sites that **antedate** the Romans' arrival in ancient Britain.

6   "The convoy's **hindmost** ship will be most vulnerable to attack," cautioned the admiral.

7   Depending on its outcome, the trial may make legal history by setting a **precedent**.

8   The meeting's **deferment** gave Luis a chance to improve his presentation.

9   To **foreshadow** the heroine's later demise, the writer kills off her dog in Chapter 1.

10   In the book's **epilogue**, the novelist hints at a forthcoming sequel.

11   "If we'd made reservations **beforehand**, we wouldn't be in this queue," grumbled Sunil.

12   Before the funeral can be held, the coroner must perform a **post-mortem**.

13   On Saturday, a protest march will **precede** the rally in the town square.

14   The events that led to the Boer War are outlined in the **foregoing** pages.

15   To honour the town's heroes, the mayor has organised a **posthumous** award ceremony.

16   "Here, the boundaries appear to **predate** Roman roads," the archaeologist noted.

17   "I've discovered the bass violin was the **antecedent** of the modern cello," remarked Gina.

18   There was no **preamble** to Jo's rant; she just started yelling.

19   Sitting in the **rearmost** row, Ollie was finding it hard to hear the actors.

20   Our Aunt Cecilia claims to be a direct **descendant** of Queen Victoria.

### Term 2: Test 21

1   **Adventuresome** people are often attracted to extreme sports.

2   With its high levels of fat and sugar, fast food is deemed **unwholesome**.

3   "Mr Stevens is so **meddlesome**! He always sticks his nose in," complained Zadie.

4   The monster's **fearsome** appearance struck terror into the heart of Beowulf.

5   "Look at this teddy bear!" enthused Zara. "It's sooo **cuddlesome**!"

6   The singer's **winsome** smile was just one of the things her fans adored.

7   A **bothersome** back injury has plagued Jumana for several weeks now.

8   With their **lithesome** movements, tigers are beautiful, if deadly, creatures.

9   Feeling **venturesome**, the yachtsman braved the Indian Ocean's turbulent waters.

10   Protected by **cumbersome** hazmat suits, the firemen approached the blazing laboratory.

11   "This is quite a **worrisome** development," admitted Beatrice.

12   One of Hercules' labours was the **loathsome** task of cleaning the Augean stables.

13   The children squealed with delight at the **gamesome** dolphins' antics.

14   At the thought of the **wearisome** trek ahead through the jungle, Brett groaned.

15   Dylan increasingly found dealing with customers' complaints every day **tiresome**.

16   "I can't watch gory zombie films; they're just too **gruesome**," Vicki confessed.

17   Unsurprisingly, the long flight had left the children irritable and **quarrelsome**.

18   The **frolicsome** fairies flitted hither and thither, singing as they went.

19   "That new vegan restaurant's food is both **wholesome** *and* tasty," raved Jim.

20   Staring at the mess, Cindy sighed at the **irksome** task of clearing it up.

### Term 2: Test 22

1   The bride's father delivered a **rambling**, yet heartfelt, speech.

2   A **discursive** argument with no clear direction will not convince readers.

3   **Abridged** versions of Charles Dickens's lengthy novels are often used in classrooms.

4   Nathan's **laconic**, monosyllabic reply infuriated his sister.

5   When summarising, be as **economical** with words as possible.

6   Frustratingly, the witness's **circuitous** account led nowhere.

7   Sula's witty brother always has an **epigrammatic** response for everything.

8   Angie, our lovely but **garrulous** neighbour, always wants to gossip.

9   "Be **concise** — I haven't got all day!" shouted the impatient bureaucrat.

10   Melanie is far more **loquacious** than her older brother, Micah.

11   My previous manager tended to address her staff in **telegraphic** bursts of words.

12   Normally quite **voluble**, Edie was strangely silent yesterday.

13   My mother regularly uses the **aphoristic** saying: "Everything comes in threes."

14   "**Meandering**, paragraph-long descriptions of nature are boring," yawned Steph.

15   Notwithstanding its **circumlocutory** start, Stan's speech was ultimately quite punchy.

16   Much praise has been lavished on the film for its **pithy** dialogue.

17   The mayoral candidate's **incisive** answers have won her new supporters.

18   Students can find a **compendious** breakdown of the syllabus in the course booklet.

19   If you tend to be **prolix**, Twitter might be the wrong platform for you.

20   Mr Gradgrind's lecture to the students was as **verbose** as it was pompous.

**Term 2: Test 23**

1  The **capillaries** are key to distributing nourishment to different parts of the body.
2  While running, Adrian tripped, tearing the **ligaments** in his left ankle.
3  The autopsy revealed a large tumour occupying much of the left **ventricle**.
4  Two of the bullets fired at the soldier were lodged in his **cranium**.
5  Crushing a person's **trachea** will prevent them from breathing, which could be fatal.
6  Falling off the ladder, Heba damaged some **cartilage** in her knee.
7  Swallowed food is carried by the **oesophagus** from the throat to the stomach.
8  Inside the lungs, the **bronchi** divide into smaller and smaller airways.
9  Sound waves are created in the **pharynx**, nose, and mouth.
10 Our **cerebrum** is responsible for our thoughts, decisions, emotions, and character.
11 Type 2 diabetes is caused by the **pancreas** not producing sufficient insulin.
12 Amazingly, a sparrow has more **vertebrae** in its neck than a giraffe!
13 The angrier Jackson grew, the more prominent the **tendons** in his neck became.
14 When Ola's **appendix** burst, she had to be rushed to hospital immediately.
15 With an inflamed **larynx**, the actor was unable to perform that night.
16 If gored by a bull, a matador may incur serious wounds to the **torso**.
17 Dr Sanjay referred to Aaron's swollen **lymph nodes** as 'buboes'.
18 To produce loud sounds, a singer has to control their **diaphragm**.
19 Leonardo da Vinci advised studying **sinews**, bones, and muscles to better depict the body.
20 Damage to the **aorta**, the body's main artery, can lead to serious complications.

**Term 2: Test 24**

1  The high levels of hissing **sibilance** rendered the old recording unusable.
2  Chan's casual **allusion** to lunch made me realise just how hungry I was.
3  **Dramatic irony** occurs when the audience knows something that the characters do not.
4  **Visual imagery** is used to evoke vivid pictures in a reader's mind.
5  Used effectively, **onomatopoeia** can conjure the typical sounds of almost any environment.
6  A silly phrase like 'as snazzy as a snail' might help you remember what a **simile** is.
7  One of the most commonly used examples of an **oxymoron** is 'bittersweet'.
8  Homer's epic, *The Odyssey*, begins with the **apostrophe**: "Sing to me of the man, Muse".
9  In Renaissance woodcuts, a grinning skeleton wielding a scythe is often the **personification** of death.
10 Famously, *Animal Farm* is an **allegory** of the Russian Revolution and its aftermath.
11 Maintaining the balance between **pathos** and comedy in a play takes much skill.
12 Shot through with **hyperbole**, Pedro's exaggerated account was wholly suspect.
13 A key challenge posed by tongue twisters is their frequent use of **alliteration**.
14 Employing 'the crown' to refer to 'the queen' is an instance of **metonymy**.
15 That poem's **aural imagery** brings it to life, eliciting the sounds of the bustling city.
16 "**Synecdoche** is a term I constantly have to look up," complained Ayah.
17 The film's sudden switch from tragedy to comedy superbly demonstrates **bathos**.
18 A phrase that illustrates **pathetic fallacy** is 'the sullen wind'.
19 Despite favouring **assonance** over rhyme, the poem remains rhythmic and musical.
20 The **metaphor** 'time flies' has become a cliché through overuse.

## Term 2: Test 25

1 To commemorate their **illustrious** statesmen, the Romans built countless monuments.

2 "You should never buy a car from a **disreputable** dealer," advised Julianna.

3 An **eminent** composer in his own time, J. S. Bach remains a giant of classical music.

4 The mere mention of the **notorious** pirate's name reduced the sailors to jelly.

5 "Such **deplorable** behaviour cannot go unpunished," uttered the magistrate.

6 The **legendary** exploits of Robin Hood fascinate people to this day.

7 Soon after being found guilty of **discreditable** financial activities, the bank closed.

8 "Your sister's **scandalous** remarks are the talk of the town," Aunt Mavis said waspishly.

9 Opinions vary widely regarding the causes of **delinquent** behaviour.

10 At various points in history, the theatre has been regarded as a **louche** environment.

11 Cheetahs are **renowned** for their remarkable speed over short distances.

12 In 1588, the Spanish Armada suffered an **ignominious** defeat at the hands of the English.

13 "Finding a **reputable** plumber is hard, but I know just the man," said Greg.

14 If you were asked to name a **celebrated** fashion designer, who would you choose?

15 "**Prominent** Hollywood stars are out in force tonight," gushed the gossip columnist.

16 "Constructive criticism is fine, but your remarks were utterly **opprobrious**," said the writer.

17 Moving in the most **exalted** social circles, Lord Montague's self-importance ballooned.

18 The colonel's insubordination resulted in his **dishonourable** discharge from the army.

19 **Leading** scientists across the world are collaborating to find a cure.

20 "It's a shame such a **distinguished** career is ending in disgrace," observed the pundit.


## Term 2: Test 26

1 Unless aimed at the right audience, an **advertorial** is completely useless.

2 The team jogged onto the pitch, their t-shirts all bearing their sponsor's **logo**.

3 Marcus has designed an eye-catching **flyer** promoting his band's next gig.

4 At the train station, a huge digital **billboard** bombarded travellers with fast food ads.

5 The company is banking on their new advertising **campaign** increasing sales.

6 "If you're to succeed, your firm needs to invest in **publicity**," the strategist remarked.

7 Appealing to people's **FOMO** is a tactic regularly employed by advertisers.

8 Tara offered to help me distribute copies of a **circular** for the new crèche.

9 Marketing experts are often consulted before the **launch** of a new product.

10 "Have you seen that glossy travel **brochure** I had?" Emilio asked.

11 Occasionally, an **endorsement** from a celebrity can backfire in unexpected ways.

12 It is ironic that many TV viewers switch off the moment an **infomercial** comes on.

13 Coming up with a distinctive **slogan** is a lot harder than you might think.

14 Outside the cinema, a man held a **placard** touting discounted DVDs.

15 "Enthralling! … Unputdownable! … Dazzling!" trumpeted the book's **blurb**.

16 "If I hear that **jingle** once more today, I'll scream," threatened Samy.

17 Over the last decade, the number of online **commercials** has gone through the roof.

18 Each conference member was given a **handout** listing local hotels and restaurants.

19 Running a **promotional** giveaway is good for raising brand awareness.

20 At one time, it was common to see a person wearing a **sandwich board** in the street.

## Term 3: Test 27

1. Recent investment has caused the city's suburbs to **burgeon**.
2. "Don't yell," advised Chloe. "It will only **exacerbate** the situation."
3. "If left unchallenged, these rumours will continue to **propagate**," warned Jed.
4. Tragically, with every passing day, the death toll continues to **mount**.
5. If Archie is to be selected for the team, he must **redouble** his efforts.
6. As soon as the doors opened, the fans began to **surge** into the venue.
7. To **accelerate** my project's progress, I asked Gita for help.
8. Rising sales encouraged the entrepreneur to **expand** his business.
9. Since the painting's value had begun to **appreciate**, the collector decided to insure it.
10. Overnight, the weeds in the garden seemed to **multiply** as if by magic.
11. Tia's criticism only served to **intensify** Ravi's stubbornness.
12. "I don't know how I've managed to **accumulate** all these plastic bags," moaned Ted.
13. "There are signs this trend will **snowball**," observed the analyst.
14. "To accommodate cruise ships, we'll have to **enlarge** the port," the engineer noted.
15. We're delighted that new shops are starting to **mushroom** in our city centre.
16. Fearing the peaceful protest would **escalate** into a riot, we decided to leave.
17. The moon is said to **wax** as it transitions from a crescent to a disc.
18. Since Gavin was having such a great time, he decided to **extend** his stay.
19. In record time, Sebastian managed to **ascend** to the rank of major.
20. "Speculations about what caused this continue to **proliferate**," announced the reporter.

## Term 3: Test 28

1. With a **grotesque** grin, the warlock began to cast his malicious spell.
2. The word '**barque**' can be used to refer to a specific kind of sailing ship.
3. Yesterday's newspaper carried a scathing **critique** of the government's new policy.
4. Famously, Mercedes-Benz is a **marque** associated with both luxury cars and F1 racing.
5. Standing motionless in the shallow water, the heron cut a **statuesque** figure.
6. To '**burlesque**' something is to parody or comically imitate it.
7. I far prefer direct disapproval to **oblique** criticism.
8. Put simply, **appliqué** involves sewing bits of fabric onto a larger piece of cloth.
9. Last summer, we rented a **picturesque** thatched cottage in Cornwall.
10. As the **goblinesque** creature began to emerge from the shadows, Petronella froze.
11. Owen's grandmother has never found his **risqué** anecdotes amusing.
12. Alicia's attempt at an **arabesque** was short-lived; she tripped over almost immediately.
13. Renaissance rulers capitalised on the **mystique** surrounding the idea of monarchy.
14. Flossing regularly can help reduce the build-up of **plaque**.
15. The heavier the vehicle, the greater its engine's **torque** needs to be.
16. The **masque** was a form of dramatic entertainment in sixteenth-century England.
17. Ornamentation and grandeur are two key characteristics of **baroque** architecture.
18. In a fit of **pique**, Stefan stormed out of the room.
19. We are expecting the War Office to issue a **communiqué** in the next few hours.
20. A **picaresque** novel is commonly formed of a series of entertaining episodes.

## Term 3: Test 29

1   Discovering that she'd won, Betty was too **flabbergasted** to speak.
2   With mouth **agape**, Callum stood stock-still, overcome with awe.
3   Camilla, who usually has an answer for everything, was **stunned** into silence.
4   Looking **dazed** and disappointed, the defeated boxer left the ring.
5   **Nonplussed** by the actor's bizarre behaviour, the audience fell silent.
6   Astrophysicists have been **confounded** by the results of the experiment.
7   Melinda laughed at the **wide-eyed** expressions on all our faces.
8   The news of the athlete's sudden retirement has left many pundits **speechless**.
9   "You look utterly **dumbstruck**!" Trudi exclaimed. "What's happened?"
10  Krista sat motionless in her chair, completely **stupefied** by her sister's tirade.
11  "'**Benumbed**' doesn't begin to describe how I feel," Luke said mournfully.
12  When I received the bill, I was **staggered** by how much I'd been charged.
13  "Prepare to be **dumbfounded**!" promised the film's rave review.
14  "Don't just sit there **goggle-eyed**!" yelled Zenobia. "Do something!"
15  "Residents remain **thunderstruck** by the devastation here," the reporter stated.
16  The story follows the fortunes of a **shell-shocked** soldier on his return from the trenches.
17  Several of us were **flummoxed** by the final question in the maths exam.
18  "I must admit to being **astounded** by Rick's apology," Vera acknowledged.
19  **Startled** by the sudden noise, the cows began stampeding in every direction.
20  Tristram didn't know what to say; the question had completely **floored** him.

## Term 3: Test 30

1   There is an expectation that oil prices will **slump** next year.
2   "Without government support, our industry will **collapse**," warned the hotelier.
3   A steady decline in profits has forced the company to **downsize**.
4   Over the years, the talented tailor's eyesight began to **deteriorate**.
5   "That sweater might **shrink** if washed in warm water," warned Darius.
6   By the fifth century, the Roman Empire's power was clearly starting to **wane**.
7   Continued poaching will **decimate** some species unless action is taken now.
8   Fascinated, Will watched the hawk **plummet** from the sky like a stone.
9   As local supplies **deplete**, we will be forced to import far more.
10  After hours of raging, the storm finally began to **abate**.
11  Hearing her mother's footsteps **recede**, Aki retrieved her phone from her bag.
12  "I refuse to let this debate **degenerate** into a slanging match," said Omar flatly.
13  Recent restrictions have forced people to **downscale** a range of cultural events.
14  "The value of these stocks is about to **plunge**," predicted the financial advisor.
15  A good project manager knows when to **devolve** responsibility to others.
16  As his popularity began to **ebb**, the actor became increasingly reclusive.
17  The king was forced to **debase** the currency to finance his costly campaign.
18  Wickets began to **tumble** as soon as the star bowler came on to the field.
19  When hot, metals expand; when cold, they **contract**.
20  As Harvey's speech dragged on, people's attention began to **dwindle**.

### Term 3: Test 31

1. Every ship is expected to fly an **ensign**: a flag that indicates nationality.
2. Within moments of swallowing the poison, the monkey began to **writhe** in agony.
3. All we know about the origin of '**ricochet**' is that it comes from 18th-century French.
4. I'm not sure how I feel about the **nascent** space tourism industry.
5. During the Renaissance, the **thumbscrew** was a favoured instrument of torture.
6. Chelsea has shocked everyone in the office by coming to work in a **psychedelic** T-shirt.
7. "There is no reason for the parties to **rescind** their agreement," averred the lawyer.
8. "Ugh! I hate it when a cold moves into the **phlegm** phase," coughed Jeff.
9. The artist's spiral patterns are inspired by a **whorl** of one of his own fingerprints.
10. Key to the band's success has been the great **rapport** between its members.
11. Every evening, tired commuters **jostle** for space on crowded trains.
12. "Sorry, we're late!" apologised Trish. "We just HAD to take the **scenic** route."
13. Logan was finding it hard not to **succumb** to the temptation of a second burger.
14. Nowadays, a **czar** is a person appointed by the government as a policy advisor.
15. Among the artefacts discovered in the vault was an exquisitely tooled **scimitar**.
16. How often do you use a **mnemonic** to remember something important?
17. Gregory's tastes are so modest that you could call them '**ascetic**'.
18. Upon his death, Prince Talbot's body was interred in the royal **sepulchre**.
19. Maria's cluttered bookshelves are home to every imaginable type of **knick-knack**.
20. Thankfully, the paramedic managed to **resuscitate** the young man.

### Term 3: Test 32

1. "That platform's user **dashboard** is totally useless!" complained Ivan.
2. Kevin's witty **hashtag** won him hundreds of new followers.
3. Sometimes, it can feel like everything we do is **algorithm**-driven.
4. Sheryll spent ages arguing that becoming an **influencer** was a good career choice.
5. "So, which **metric** should I be focusing on?" asked the manager.
6. "I disliked statistics at school. Imagine how I feel about **analytics**!" Gina commented.
7. Adding a **geotag** can help make your photos more discoverable.
8. "I wanted to **repost** this, but I couldn't see how to do it," grumbled Chan.
9. Marco never customizes his **avatar** on any of his social media accounts.
10. "On average, how many daily **impressions** do your posts receive?" inquired the marketer.
11. Levels of **engagement** with content are determined by a wide range of factors.
12. Randall had to spend several hours **archiving** old articles on his blog.
13. It would be nice to think people have become less susceptible to **clickbait**.
14. "Why not apply a **filter** to your photo to make it pop more?" Juan suggested.
15. Using **crowdsourcing** to answer a question can yield some intriguing results.
16. I was thrilled that there was going to be a **live stream** of my favourite fashion show.
17. A defining characteristic of a **Bitmoji** is that it is customisable.
18. "I HATE accidentally deleting a **notification** before I've read it properly!" groaned Mia.
19. Caroline seems incapable of sending me an **emoji**-free text message.
20. "When you **favourite** a video, do you also leave a comment?" inquired the pollster.

## Term 3: Test 33

1  Due to the **sparsity** of food, the besieged citizens were forced to surrender.
2  Facing **destitution**, Fiona swallowed her pride and asked her wealthy aunt for help.
3  A '**blight**' is a disease that affects plants and is typically caused by bacteria or fungi.
4  "We will find ourselves in dire **straits** unless we act now," insisted Arvind.
5  Having skipped breakfast, Katrina was **famished** by lunchtime.
6  One major challenge the early settlers had to face was the **barrenness** of the land.
7  Countries with a **paucity** of natural resources often import diverse raw materials.
8  The **meagreness** of many people's salaries means they enjoy few luxuries.
9  Distressed by the number of people in **want**, Selma volunteered at a local charity.
10 Sadly, significant **deprivation** is a common feature of life in a shanty town.
11 "Sire," said the sultan's advisor gravely, "this **pestilence** is ravaging your people."
12 The unseasonal **drought** has resulted in many vital crops being lost.
13 In 2021, the global scarcity of chips led to the **undersupply** of many consumer electronics.
14 I know I shouldn't have been surprised by the **aridity** of the Sahara, but I was.
15 This year's rice **shortage** is being blamed on insufficient rainfall.
16 The **privation** of food was a major contributing factor to the expedition's failure.
17 During WWII, rationing was made inevitable by the **dearth** of essential food items.
18 "More and more people will face **starvation** if things don't change," said the campaigner.
19 "You know, a **lack** of water is probably why your flowers died," commented Raja.
20 Investment in aquaculture could yet help avert a **catastrophe** in wild fisheries.

## Term 3: Test 34

1  Often **antagonistic** towards each other, ancient Greek city states frequently went to war.
2  In view of the current rail strike, intercity travel has become **problematic**.
3  Lorries are fitted with **hydraulic** brakes because of their reliability.
4  "I've recently taken up sketching and am finding it quite **therapeutic**," Regina told me.
5  An **analgesic** such as paracetamol can help reduce swelling.
6  Banksy's **idiosyncratic** style has made his works highly sought after.
7  During the 1970s, **quadraphonic** sound systems were all the rage.
8  "Can't you find a word to use *other* than '**neurotic**'?" snapped Luis.
9  In mythology, a **chimeric** creature is one formed from the parts of several animals.
10 The praise being lavished on her debut novel is nothing short of **rhapsodic**.
11 A whistle-blower has released evidence of the company's **systemic** criminal negligence.
12 '**Elliptic**' is one of those adjectives to which you can further add the suffix '-al'.
13 The names of many famous orchestras contain the word '**philharmonic**'.
14 Louisa marvelled at the **eclectic** mix of antiques and modern art in the gallery.
15 "Is it true that cherries have a **soporific** effect and can make you sleepy?" Angie asked.
16 Overwhelmed by Jumana's **empathetic** response, Pablo burst into tears.
17 Just because a person is **stoic** doesn't mean they are without feelings.
18 "Classical physics defines energy as **kinetic** energy or potential energy," she explained.
19 With a diplomat for a mother, Luna has led quite a **peripatetic** childhood.
20 Professor Wilson's students either loved or loathed her **sardonic** wit.

## Term 3: Test 35

1. Notwithstanding Raj's fears, his driving test passed without **mishap**.
2. Attempting to convince Bob he is wrong is like talking to a **brick wall**.
3. "Don't **stonewall**," ordered Maria. "Answer the question right now!"
4. Julia has always found gloves an **encumbrance** when doing the washing-up.
5. Showing great **restraint**, Mona resisted the offer of more pasta.
6. During the Cold War, the principle of nuclear **deterrence** was widely debated.
7. Selma's knee injury has proven a major **setback** to her training programme.
8. What would you say is the greatest **barrier** to effective communication?
9. "As far as I can see, the only **hurdle** will be getting Anita to agree," commented Igor.
10. Before the trial, the judge ordered an **embargo** on the taking of photographs in court.
11. Once children overcome their shyness, you may find they talk with less **constraint**.
12. 'Without let or **hindrance**' is a formal way of saying 'without obstruction'.
13. Our project didn't go according to plan; in fact, we hit a **snag** right at the start.
14. Campaigners fear the new laws will be an **impediment** to securing justice for victims.
15. Vincent has been working hard to **curb** his tendency to be sarcastic.
16. "Come on, guys!" yelled Aiko impatiently. "What's the **hold-up**?"
17. "I've been told the power **stoppage** has lasted over a week," said the reporter.
18. In some sports, a **handicap** is imposed on superior players to make things fairer.
19. Last week, an **obstruction** on the track delayed our train to Leeds.
20. One **drawback** to buying lots of books is that you soon run out of shelf space.

## Term 3: Test 36

1. "So," said the detective, producing a **snapshot**, "how do you explain this?"
2. **High-resolution** screens display images in an incredible amount of detail.
3. "'**Overexposure**' means an image has been in the light too long," said the instructor.
4. "I often use a **contact sheet** to review a collection of images," the photographer stated.
5. To maximise the brightness of a shot, the lens **aperture** should be widened.
6. "For me, **sepia**-toned photographs conjure up the late nineteenth century," he said.
7. In Photoshop, the **foreground** colour can be changed using the Eyedropper tool.
8. "Isn't being a **camera-shy** celebrity a contradiction in terms?" Wanda pondered.
9. Curiously, good looks do not automatically mean a person is **photogenic**.
10. Barging into the **darkroom**, Ken let in the light and ruined Hal's photos.
11. While people might think **photobombing** is a recent trend, it's been around for years.
12. "Applying effects to **low-resolution** images can have interesting results," observed Laila.
13. The use of **digital zoom** may compromise the quality of an image.
14. High-definition **close-up** images can be used to create detailed textures.
15. Hearing the **flashbulb** pop, the recluse realised his picture had just been taken.
16. As far as we know, the earliest use of the term '**camera obscura**' dates to 1604.
17. Adding **grain** to an image can help give it a more vintage look.
18. A **negative** is an image in which the light areas appear dark, and vice versa.
19. Alonzo couldn't believe that Arla had never taken a **selfie**.
20. The **exposure** of an undeveloped black and white film roll to light will ruin it.

### Term 3: Test 37

1  To emphasise his point, the journalist has used a **quotation** from *Hamlet*.
2  Today's **editorial** launched a scathing attack on the government's proposed budget.
3  In the pre-digital era, **typesetting** was a laborious, manual process.
4  The purpose of a **byline** is to identify the writer of an article.
5  My editor has insisted on the **redaction** of several sentences in my report.
6  At the start of his career, Alexis worked in advertising as a **copywriter**.
7  As the word suggests, a '**photojournalist**' communicates news stories through images.
8  "Every **headline** is more depressing than the last," noted Irene dolefully.
9  Not all web editions of **broadsheet** newspapers are free to access.
10  One of the borough councillors is suing a newspaper for publishing a **misquotation**.
11  Although used interchangeably, the terms '**font**' and 'typeface' are not the same.
12  I'm not sure if I like the recent changes to that paper's **layout**.
13  "10 pages of exclusive eyewitness accounts," promised the **strapline**.
14  Yesterday, our local paper printed a **retraction** for an error in its Friday edition.
15  "In the age of the internet, **fact-checking** is ever more crucial," the academic stated.
16  One characteristic of the **tabloid** press is celebrity gossip.
17  "I detest **proofreading**," complained Nina. "It always takes so long to do properly!"
18  For years, Mrs Sanders wrote an agony aunt **column** for a well-known magazine.
19  Newspaper reporters were first referred to as '**the fourth estate**' in 1843.
20  A newspaper's circulation is calculated based on its average daily **distribution**.

### Term 3: Test 38

1  Once their financial records were audited, the level of **fraudulence** became apparent.
2  "The **covertness** of this mission is central to its success," stated the general.
3  "We need a new **stratagem** to deal with this," Zhao said decisively.
4  "All this **double-dealing** will catch up with you eventually," cautioned Tina.
5  Desperate to regain his throne, the deposed king **intrigued** with his loyal nobles.
6  The extent of her **mendacity** has shocked and disappointed us all.
7  Growing weary of his own **dissimulation**, Mr Darcy finally admitted his feelings.
8  People have become jaded by all the recent political **chicanery**.
9  "How has our pharmacy been a **smokescreen** for money laundering?" gasped Shona.
10  "I don't believe a word," snorted Ivy. "You have been **dissembling** the whole time."
11  With a surprising lack of **artifice**, the salesperson highlighted the product's flaws.
12  As a child, Amira loved reading tales of pirates and their **skulduggery**.
13  '**Cozenage**' is a late sixteenth-century word meaning 'trickery'.
14  Identifying where truth ends and **falsehood** begins can be complicated sometimes.
15  "Considerable **guile** went into staging this hacking," observed the analyst.
16  Catalina was unimpressed by her sister's **machinations** to fool their parents.
17  The vizier hid his **duplicity** well and, as such, misled many people.
18  "Be done with your **subterfuge**; tell me the truth," she commanded.
19  Lucilla kicked herself for having been taken in so easily by Pete's **deception**.
20  "It was the **furtiveness** of his behaviour that first made me suspicious," said Kay.

## Term 3: Test 39

1. The latest blockbuster is a **hotchpotch** of unresolved plot lines and 2D characters.
2. Tina loves Halloween: the costumes, the pumpkins, the horror films — the whole **caboodle**.
3. "Fantasy fiction? Pah!" scoffed Monique. "It's all utter **piffle**!"
4. The word '**murmuration**' can be used as a collective noun for starlings.
5. "Gentlemen, **fisticuffs** are not allowed on the premises," said the club owner sternly.
6. "Don't be such a **nincompoop**!" exclaimed Fred. "Of course, we're still friends!"
7. "He never makes any sense; all he ever spouts is **codswallop**," she complained.
8. "So," Santa said to his elves, "what **shenanigans** have you been up to in my absence?"
9. "I refuse to **kowtow** to the imposter!" declared the princess stoutly.
10. "Your lies will not **obfuscate** the truth," stated the sheriff. "I know you betrayed me."
11. A '**flibbertigibbet**' is a person who talks excessively, or who is frivolous and irresponsible.
12. "The meal was an inedible **mishmash** of Japanese and Italian cuisines," declared Fran.
13. Falling for the old **switcheroo**, Disa was conned into buying a fake designer handbag.
14. I know it's a bit unfair, but bulldogs always seem to have **lugubrious** faces.
15. "Don't be such a **namby-pamby**!" scolded Omar. "You didn't bash yourself *that* hard!"
16. "Your attempts to **discombobulate** me aren't working," said Paolo smugly.
17. "Ooh, look! Your cat's eyeing the last **titbit** on your plate," chuckled Alicia.
18. "I can't believe it," said Dido, shaking her head. "Juno is running the whole **shebang**."
19. According to Greek mythology, **ichor**, not blood, ran in the veins of the gods.
20. "What are you trying to do?" interrupted Rita rudely. "Stage a **filibuster**?"

# SUGGESTED ANSWERS

To help you, we have provided a selection of possible answers to the student prompts included in the units (e.g. the Vocabulary Builders, Synonym Spottings, & Can You Think Ofs).

**Please note, however, that these answers are intended as guidelines only.**
Students may well come up with alternative, correct answers of their own.

## #1 WWI (p. 5)
**Vocabulary Builder**
Ships-related words: convoy | dreadnought | U-boat
Specific names for soldiers: artillery | doughboy | infantry

**Can You Think Of...**
Homophones: draft & draught
Homonyms: draft (*n.* conscription) & draft (*v.* to prepare an initial version of a text)

## #2 That Doesn't Look Right... (p. 7)
**Vocabulary Builder**
Nouns: atheist | dilemma | idiosyncrasy | kernel | millennium | omission | pavilion | perseverance | personnel
Verbs: concede | exhilarate | harass | indict | inoculate | supersede
Adjectives: humorous | outrageous

**Can You Think Of...**
Homophones: gauge & gage | kernel & colonel

## #3 As Dull As Ditchwater (p. 9)
**Vocabulary Builder**
Adjectives used to describe writing: pedestrian | prosaic | undramatic | unimaginative

**Synonym Spotting**
dreary = tedious (*i.e. monotonous*)

## #4 Breaking the Law (p. 11)
**Synonym Spotting**
pickpocket = petty thief | vandal = hooligan

## #5 From Benediction to Malodorous (p. 13)

Synonym & Antonym Soup
Illness: malady = malaise | Un/kind: malignant ≠ benign

**Vocabulary Builder**
Types of people: benefactor | benefactress | beneficiary | malcontent | malefactor

## #6 Total Bedlam (p. 15)
**Vocabulary Builder**
Words of Greek/Latin origin: anarchy | chaos | commotion | furore | pandemonium

## #7 Eureka! (p. 17)
**Vocabulary Builder**
Closed compound words: brainchild | brainstorm | brainwave

**Synonym Spotting**
perception = discernment | deduction = inference

## #8 Double Trouble (p. 19)
**Vocabulary Builder**
Specific types of people: intelligentsia | supplicant | connoisseur

## #9 James Bond & Co. (p. 21)
**Vocabulary Builder**
Names of people engaged in espionage: handler | insider | mole

**Synonym & Antonym Soup**
reconnaissance = exploration | deceit ≠ honesty

## #10 Rags to Riches (p. 23)
**Synonym & Antonym Soup**
bankrupt = insolvent | impecunious ≠

affluent

**Can You Think Of...**
Homophones: straitened & straightened

## #11 Happy Endings I (p. 25)
**Vocabulary Builder**
Personal relationships-related words:
courtship | fellowship | kinship | partnership
Jobs-related words: apprenticeship |
internship | leadership | ownership |
partnership | workmanship

## #12 Make an Impact (p. 27)
**Vocabulary Builder**
Captivation-related words: alluring | beguiled
| charismatically | enticingly | hypnotic |
riveting

## #13 That Said... (p. 29)
**Synonym & Antonym Soup**
above all = chiefly | undoubtedly ≠
questionably

## #14 Newton's Cradle (p. 31)
**Can You Think Of...**
Homophones: current & currant
Homonyms: current (*n.* a flow of electricity)
& current (*adj.* relating or belonging to the
present)

## #15 Hypercritical or Hypocritical? (p. 33)
**Vocabulary Builder**
Adjectives used to describe people:
hyperactive | hypercritical | hypersensitive |
hypocritical

**Antonym Alert**
hypercritical ≠ easy-going | hypocrisy ≠
sincerity

## #17 Justice is Served (p. 37)
**Vocabulary Builder**
People who pass judgement: arbitrator | jury
| magistrate

**Synonym & Antonym Soup**

accusation = allegation | hearsay ≠ facts

## #18 Head-Scratchers (p. 39)
**Vocabulary Builder**
Literature-related words: censor | cite |
satire

## #19 Kaput! (p. 41)
**Vocabulary Builder**
Food-related words: delicatessen | muesli |
pretzel

## #21 Happy Endings II (p. 45)
**Synonym & Antonym Soup**
bothersome = irritating | cumbersome ≠
efficient

**Vocabulary Builder**
Positive adjectives for people:
adventuresome | gamesome | winsome

## #22 Short & Sweet vs Long-Winded (p. 47)
**Vocabulary Builder**
Adjectives for talkative people: garrulous |
loquacious | verbose | voluble

## #23 Body Language (p. 49)
**Vocabulary Builder**
The respiratory system: bronchi | larynx |
pharynx | trachea

## #24 Figuratively Speaking... (p. 51)
**Vocabulary Builder**
Broad classifications for poetic use of
language: aural imagery | visual imagery

**Can You Think Of...**
Homonyms: apostrophe (*n.* figure of speech)
& apostrophe (*n.* punctuation mark)
Homophones: aural & oral

## #25 Claim to Fame (p. 53)
**Synonym & Antonym Soup**
distinguished = renowned | reputable ≠
louche

### #26 BOGOF (p. 55)
**Vocabulary Builder**
Words related to TV, radio, or streaming advertising: commercials | jingle

### #27 A Rapid Rise... (p. 57)
**Vocabulary Builder**
Number-related words: multiply | proliferate | redouble

### #28 Que-ing Up (p. 59)
**Vocabulary Builder**
Nouns with multiple definitions:
plaque (1): a commemorative tablet made of stone, metal, etc. that is fixed to a flat surface
plaque (2): a substance containing bacteria that forms on the surface of teeth

torque (1): a force that causes rotation
torque (2): a neck ornament

**Can You Think Of...**
Homophones: barque & bark | pique & peek OR pique & peak

### #29 S is for Surprised (p. 61)
**Vocabulary Builder**
Face-related words: agape | goggle-eyed | wide-eyed

### #30 ...Or A Slow Decline? (p. 63)
**A. About these Words...**
Possible antonym pairs: contract ≠ expand | slump ≠ surge | wane ≠ wax

**Vocabulary Builder**
Words related to businesses: collapse | downscale | downsize

**Synonym Spotting**
dwindle = wane | ebb = recede | plummet = plunge

### #31 Silent, but Deadly (p. 65)
**Vocabulary Builder**
The body: phlegm | whorl

**Can You Think Of...**
Homophones: whorl & whirl

### #32 It's Gone Viral (p. 67)
**Vocabulary Builder**
Interaction-related word: favourite
Data-related words: analytics | archiving | geotag

### #33 Going Without (p. 69)
**Can You Think Of...**
Homonyms: straits (*n.* a narrow passage, usually of water) & straits (*n.* difficulties)

### #34 Happy Endings III (p. 71)
**Vocabulary Builder**
Physics: elliptic | hydraulic | kinetic

### #35 A Fly in the Ointment (p. 73)
**Can You Think Of...**
Homophones: curb & kerb

### #36 Say Cheese! (p. 75)
**Vocabulary Builder**
Closed compound words: darkroom | flashbulb | photobombing | snapshot

### #37 Stop the Presses! (p. 77)
**Vocabulary Builder**
Further related compound words: photojournalism | proofreader | typesetter

### #38 T is for Trickery (p. 79)
**Vocabulary Builder**
Lying: falsehood | mendacity
Cunning: chicanery | guile

### #39 That's a Proper Word?!?! (p. 81)
**Vocabulary Builder**
Nonsense: codswallop | piffle

**Synonym Spotting**
kowtow = grovel | lugubrious = gloomy

# INDEX I

*This index organizes the units in this workbook according to their target areas. The entries in each main category are listed in alphabetical order.*

## SPELLING PATTERNS

**Commonly Mistaken Spellings:** #2 That Doesn't Look Right... (p. 7)

**Doubled Consonants:** #8 Double Trouble (p. 19)

**Homophones & Near Homophones:** #18 Head-Scratchers (p. 39)

**Silent Letters:** #31 Silent, but Deadly (p. 65)

**Suffix -ic:** #34 Happy Endings III (p. 71)
**Suffix -ship:** #11 Happy Endings I (p. 25)
**Suffix -some:** #21 Happy Endings II (p. 45)

**Words beginning with ben/e- & mal/e-:** #5 From Benediction to Malodorous (p. 13)
**Words beginning with hyper- & hypo-:** #15 Hypercritical or Hypocritical? (p. 33)
**Words ending with -que:** #28 Que-ing Up (p. 59)

**Words from Other Languages: German:** #19 Kaput! (p. 41)

## THEMED AREAS OF GENERAL KNOWLEDGE

**Advertising:** #26 BOGOF (p. 55)
**Famine & Related Shortages:** #33 Going Without (p. 69)
**Newspapers:** #37 Stop the Presses! (p. 77)
**Parts of the Human Body:** #23 Body Language (p. 49)
**Photography:** #36 Say Cheese! (p. 75)
**Physics:** #14 Newton's Cradle (p. 31)
**Social Media:** #32 It's Gone Viral (p. 67)
**Spies & Espionage:** #9 James Bond & Co. (p. 21)
**The Law: Courtrooms:** #17 Justice is Served (p. 37)
**The Law: Types of Criminals** #4 Breaking the Law (p. 11)
**World War I:** #1 WWI (p. 5)

## USEFUL VOCABULARY: SYNONYMS & ANTONYMS

**Synonyms: 'Boring':** #3 As Dull As Ditchwater (p. 9)
**Synonyms: 'Chaos':** #6 Total Bedlam (p. 15)
**Synonyms: 'Decrease':** #30 ...Or A Slow Decline? (p. 63)
**Synonyms: 'Increase':** #27 A Rapid Rise... (p. 57)
**Synonym & Antonym Set: Exactness vs Digression:** #22 Short & Sweet vs Long-Winded (p. 47)
**Synonym & Antonym Set: Lucky vs Unlucky:** #16 Luck of the Draw (p. 35)
**Synonym & Antonym Set: Poverty vs Wealth:** #10 Rags to Riches (p. 23)

## USEFUL VOCABULARY: WORD CLUSTERS

**Word Cluster: Ideas:** #7 Eureka! (p. 17)
**Word Cluster: Obstruction:** #35 A Fly in the Ointment (p. 73)
**Word Cluster: Prior & Post:** #20 Before... & After (p. 43)
**Word Cluster: Surprise:** #29 S is for Surprised (p. 61)
**Word Cluster: Trickery:** #38 T is for Trickery (p. 79)

## WORDS FOR CREATIVE WRITING, FORMAL WRITING, & TEXTUAL ANALYSIS

**Fun Words:** #39 That's a Proper Word?!?! (p. 81)
**Good Reputation vs Bad Reputation:** #25 Claim to Fame (p. 53)
**Power Words:** #12 Make an Impact (p. 27)

**Useful Linking Words & Phrases:** #13 That Said... (p. 29)

**Figures of Speech:** #24 Figuratively Speaking... (p. 51)

# INDEX II

*This index lists the units in order with a brief key to the area each unit targets.*

## TERM 1

**#1 WWI (p. 5):** Themed: World War I

**#2 That Doesn't Look Right... (p. 7):** Spelling Patterns: Commonly Mistaken Spellings

**#3 As Dull As Ditchwater (p. 9):** Vocabulary: Synonyms: Boring

**#4 Breaking the Law (p. 11):** Themed: The Law: Types of Criminals

**#5 From Benediction to Malodorous (p. 13):** Spelling Patterns: Words beginning with ben/e- & mal/e-

**#6 Total Bedlam (p. 15):** Vocabulary: Synonyms: Chaos

**#7 Eureka! (p. 17):** Vocabulary: Word Cluster: Ideas

**#8 Double Trouble (p. 19):** Spelling Patterns: Doubled Consonants

**#9 James Bond & Co. (p. 21):** Themed: Spies & Espionage

**#10 Rags to Riches (p. 23):** Vocabulary: Synonym & Antonym Set: Poverty vs Wealth

**#11 Happy Endings I (p. 25):** Spelling Patterns: Suffix -ship

**#12 Make an Impact (p. 27):** Creative Writing: Power Words

**#13 That Said... (p. 29):** Formal Writing: Useful Linking Words & Phrases

## TERM 2

**#14 Newton's Cradle (p. 31):** Themed: Physics

**#15 Hypercritical or Hypocritical? (p. 33):** Spelling Patterns: Words beginning with hyper- & hypo-

**#16 Luck of the Draw (p. 35):** Vocabulary: Synonym & Antonym Set: Lucky vs Unlucky

**#17 Justice is Served (p. 37):** Themed: The Law: Courtrooms

**#18 Head-Scratchers (p. 39):** Spelling Patterns: Homophones & Near Homophones

**#19 Kaput! (p. 41):** Spelling Patterns: Words from Other Languages: German

**#20 Before... & After (p. 43):** Vocabulary: Word Cluster: Prior & Post

**#21 Happy Endings II (p. 45):** Spelling Patterns: Suffix -some

**#22 Short & Sweet vs Long-Winded (p. 47):** Vocabulary: Synonym & Antonym Set: Exactness vs Digression

**#23 Body Language (p. 49):** Themed: Parts of the Human Body

**#24 Figuratively Speaking... (p. 51):** Textual Analysis: Figures of Speech

**#25 Claim to Fame (p. 53):** Creative Writing: Good Reputation vs Bad Reputation

**#26 BOGOF (p. 55):** Themed: Advertising

## TERM 3

**#27 A Rapid Rise... (p. 57):** Vocabulary: Synonyms: Increase

**#28 Que-ing Up (p. 59):** Spelling Patterns: Words ending with -que

**#29 S is for Surprised (p. 61):** Vocabulary: Word Cluster: Surprise

**#30 ...Or A Slow Decline? (p. 63):** Vocabulary: Synonyms: Decrease

**#31 Silent, but Deadly (p. 65):** Spelling Patterns: Silent Letters

**#32 It's Gone Viral (p. 67):** Themed: Social Media

**#33 Going Without (p. 69):** Themed: Famine & Related Shortages

**#34 Happy Endings III (p. 71):** Spelling Patterns: Suffix -ic

**#35 A Fly in the Ointment (p. 73):** Vocabulary: Word Cluster: Obstruction

**#36 Say Cheese! (p. 75):** Themed: Photography

**#37 Stop the Presses! (p. 77):** Themed: Newspapers

**#38 T is for Trickery (p. 79):** Vocabulary: Word Cluster: Trickery

**#39 That's a Proper Word?!?! (p. 81):** Creative Writing: Fun Words

Made in the USA
Las Vegas, NV
17 August 2023

76226383R00063